My mission and my passion is to serve the needs of you, your loved ones and a nation as a whole. I am here to reveal to you the tools you already possess to make this decision and take control of your future today.

Lisa Christiansen is the global authority on Leadership Psychology and human behavior, Dr. Lisa Christiansen has helped millions of people create extraordinary lives globally. Her expertise and guidance has enriched the lives of icons such as pop superstar Kelly Clarkson, rock legend Journey Olympian Dara Torres, and Super Star Patrick Dempsey.

Are you ready to live life on your terms? Your Journey Starts here.

Thank you for choosing me to walk beside you on your journey to success!

With Love and Gratitude,
Dr. Lisa Christine Christiansen

Do You Suffer From Status Anxiety?

A study recently came out that says [Darwin may have been wrong](#) about "survival of the fittest". This information came from researchers at the University of Bristol in England that was published in [Biology Letters](#). They say finding the right "living space" may be more important than [natural selection](#). Of course, there are many other scientists charging that the data this study is based on is being misinterpreted. Or that perhaps, even that the data itself is wrong. What it does support for me, is how it is really important for people to ensure they find the right "pond" to live in... This refers to both your physical "pond" and those with whom you spend your time.

Today, people feel a lot of unnecessary and unneeded stress caused by comparing themselves to others. This stress puts a toll on both their mental and physical health. In fact, even the [CDC](#) says that ["emotional health" can be up to 85% responsible for physical health](#).

First, you must understand that your physical surroundings determine who you "hang" with and who you "hang" with is a large determinant of your self-worth. You are a reflection of your five closest friends. This is because we as social creatures tend to base our opinions of ourselves on comparisons between ourselves and those in our immediate circles. This can work both for you and against you. Surrounding yourself with others who have achieved things – and a [level of success](#) – you desire to achieve, gives you examples after which to model your behavior.

Mark 11:24 Therefore I tell you, whatever you ask for in prayer, believe that you have received it, and it will be yours.

On the other hand, if you are constantly comparing yourselves to these people, that can cause you immense stress. Thus, this is a highly individualized matter that you must consider on a personal level and how these comparisons affect you in particular.

Some people need to be "reaching up" to be motivated. While others need to excel within their personal group to feel confident enough to eventually reach up. It is a fine balance. That is why we will be examining this subject over the next couple of weeks from both angles but we'll hit on a quick summary now…

If you are one who gets stressed by comparing yourself to your more successful friends, neighbors, or co-workers, one of the quickest ways to change any negative feelings, jealousy, or status envy you might have is to ensure you also have people who are at your current socio-economic and enviro-economic status in your circle as well.

This idea was put forth in "[How to Get Over Status Anxiety](#)" at [www.psychologytoday.com](#). This is not to imply that you necessarily change your circle of friends. It's just that you need to be more conscientious of who you compare yourself to on a regular basis.

For example, you can seek out those you can better and more appropriate identify with through social and civic groups. And sometimes, one can better flourish by seeking out "smaller settings" in which to work and play as well. Sometimes successes are easier to come by and recognize in such a setting. You must also learn to recognize your own successes - in their own right - and use them to balance what you feel are you failures or shortcomings that only exist in comparison to others.

Mark 11:24 Therefore I tell you, whatever you ask for in prayer, believe that you have received it, and it will be yours.

Especially comparisons to others who might have more advantages - or resources - than you do at your disposal.

Perhaps most importantly, learn to use this "envy" for good. Use it to propel you to greater heights. Instead of thinking, "Poor me. I don't have..." or "I'll never be able to do what so-and-so did because I didn't grow up rich" or "I'm not as educated so I am not as smart as...", and letting those things get you down on yourself, begin to consider how your particular circumstances served you. Only you have the power to decide that. Has a lack of certain things in your life forced you to be resourceful? Has your lack of money in your life put you in a position to empathize with those facing certain problems that only you - with your underprivileged or even middle-class background - can really understand? Maybe your lack of formal education has driven you to really study the world - or independently - so that you actually have more practical knowledge than your more "classroom educated" counterparts?

On the other hand, if you are someone who needs to be consistently challenged to strive for "more", then add people to your circle of influence who are currently where you desire to be and mirror them. This will take years off your journey to success and allow you to arrive at your destination in a much shorter time. There are always two sides to every coin and while some need to remain secure in their current situation – and there is nothing wrong with that if that is what gives you greater emotional security and satisfaction – I, on the other hand, am always searching for growth.

I believe that wherever you are at some point in time, you have made an "appointment" to be there. Being

Mark 11:24 Therefore I tell you, whatever you ask for in prayer, believe that you have received it, and it will be yours.

"wealthy" isn't just a question of how much money you have, but rather having what you want. It has been said by many that success without fulfillment is failure. Wealth isn't absolute, it's relative to desire... SELF ESTEEM= success divided by expectation. Meaning, people base their self-worth on their definition of success. To be successful, one must be prepared for opportunity and then answer the door when it knocks – or lower your expectation – either way decide what works for you.

For today, the key here is remembering that everything in life serves you equally. Aside from the other practical steps mentioned above, your attitude - and view - on these things, can change your life as much as (or more!) than anything. For the next few weeks, we will cover this more intricately. In the meantime, remember that success – for you – is merely a matter of how you define it. What is your definition of "success"?

Mark 11:24 Therefore I tell you, whatever you ask for in prayer, believe that you have received it, and it will be yours.

Mark 11:24 Therefore I tell you, whatever you ask for in prayer, believe that you have received it, and it will be yours.

Money Can't Buy Happiness... Or Can't it?

I read an interesting story in Wired today. The name of the article was "*Why Money Can't Buy Happiness*" by Jonah Lehrer.

The general theme of this piece is explaining why America - the richest nation of this century - is growing more and more unhappy...the richer we get.

This is exactly opposite of what most people believe. There is a general idea among the masses that they will be happy "*when...*".

A very frequent version of that sentence is, *"When I have money..."*

Yet, this article reports scientists have proven when an average individual actually starts *manifesting more money* and *amassing greater wealth*, they start indulging in the "finer things" in life. This, in turn, causes them to lose their ability to appreciate **life's small (daily) treasures**.

Where do you fall in this discussion? Do you believe *money can create happiness*? Or do you believe *money is actually the root of all evil*, causing one to become bored with - and miss - the "*little things*" that used to make you happy?

Despite what these scientists have "*proven*", I have to say that neither of these answers is absolutely correct. **Money in and of itself will not make you happy**. Being able to buy everything you want, stay at the finest places, live in the grandest house... Yes, all those things will cause momentary "*highs*" but after a

Mark 11:24 Therefore I tell you, whatever you ask for in prayer, believe that you have received it, and it will be yours.

while, they just become "*things*".

On the other hand, money is not evil either. It cannot - all by itself - turn a person "*bad*". This literally depends **on your relationship with money** and what you do with it once you have it. If you use money to **enrich your life** - and **enrich the lives of others** - it can bring you great joy. If you respect money, and only spend your money on things that bring you joy because they touch your heart and spirit, *money can enrich your life*. It's all about perspective.

One thing is certain, however, no matter what... You will never have money if you don't have a healthy respect for both its power for good and it's power for destruction. **Once you balance that relationship, you will find money flows to you freely and easily.**

Therefore, if "*more money*" is something you want in your life, don't be alarmed by this study. Simply take a few moments and figure out *why* you want **more money** and what you will do with it once you have it. Then, once you know you *won't* take it for granted - or abuse it - when it comes to you, you will find you have access to *more money – more riches –* than you ever imagined.

Mark 11:24 Therefore I tell you, whatever you ask for in prayer, believe that you have received it, and it will be yours.

Mark 11:24 Therefore I tell you, whatever you ask for in prayer, believe that you have received it, and it will be yours.

8 Secrets to Wealth Creation

Do you want to live in wealth? These are the 8 secrets that all masters of wealth have in common; do you have what it takes?

Wealth Creation Secret No. 1:

I know one thing for sure and two things for certain... To create exponential wealth today, you must own your own business and here are the two reasons why.

Your belief may be that the corporate executive with the $100,000 a year job has a net worth more than the small shop owner, but the truth of the matter is that the executive will be challenged to double his/her income and with the expenses of having a family this will limit the amount of savings not to mention that the taxes will eat up most of any profits that are left.

What I have found through my own personal experience is that the smallest home business owner has unlimited opportunities to expand his/her business and income, as well as how many employees, in most cases the owner is even able to write their own paychecks, and has the control to increase sales whenever they choose. Did I mention they also have time freedom?

Wealth Creation Secret No. 2.

Remember the three levels of mastery

1. Cognitive Mastery: understand what you have learned.
2. Emotional Mastery: Link what you learn to emotions
3. Physical Mastery: you have done enough repetition to make it natural, now anchor these together!

You must be passionate enough to have a working knowledge of your chosen business when you start and continue to take steps to be a professional student expanding your knowledge as you master your skills (it is better to live by example than to lead by ignorance).

What I have learned through my personal and professional life experiences is that If you don't know what you're doing your mistakes will be many as well as costly and more often than not unnecessary, and you will not be able to keep up with the ever growing technologies in any field. Start smart and stay that way. Information linked to emotion is retained.

Wealth Creation Secret No. 3.

Saving money in your personal life and in your business venture is equally as important.

Always remember it is not how much you make when you are right it is how much you save when you are wrong. Self discipline is the key to saving money. You must develop the will power to deny yourself instant gratification or the temptation of the "get rich quick" thinking. Resources will be needed for growth and should be guarded carefully.

Mitigate your risks and always protect yourself.

Mark 11:24 Therefore I tell you, whatever you ask for in prayer, believe that you have received it, and it will be yours.

Wealth Creation Secret No. 4.

You must take risks with borrowed money, your own money or both. Your number one resource is your resourcefulness.

Taking risks is essential to the growth of your business. Some of the richest women and men have staked their entire life savings and lost, several times over, before the risk-taking paid off.

When you back risks with good judgment, experience, commitment, and the right support you have a formula for wealth creation. Now the most important step is to follow through and follow up. Did I mention follow up?...

Search out others for advice on risk taking from the wealthy who still take calculated risks with successful returns, not from your friends who risk nothing more than a few bucks on a lottery ticket and remember you are your top 5 friends so think about that and seek wisely.

Wealth Creation Secret No. 5.

Do you know the difference between a piece of coal and a diamond? YES, the answer is pressure! Right now you are a diamond in the rough; you just need a little more pressure...

It is important to not only learn to live with tension, you must passionately seek it out.

Learn to thrive on stress! begin getting physically fit, have a psychological overhaul and ingrain new anchors. What will it take for you to handle it? Start now!

Mark 11:24 Therefore I tell you, whatever you ask for in prayer, believe that you have received it, and it will be yours.

Once you make the decision to thrive on stress, you will enjoy it, you will begin seeking it out willingly and enthusiastically and wonder how you ever lived any other way.

Women and men of wealth look at making money as a game much like a child playing monopoly of which they love to play passionately.

Think about this… your biggest problem isn't that you don't know what you don't know it's that you don't know what you do know.

Keep things in perspective and you will be in control of your stress level, once you learn to master your emotions you will be in control of your life. What will it feel like to live life on your terms?

Perception is everything, we give things meaning. You decide what things mean.

Information linked to emotion is retained.

Wealth Creation Secret No. 6.

Create wealth as a positive side effect of your business success.

If money is your only outcome in business, you will more than likely fail.

The money is the bonus of the game. If you win, the money will be there.

Remember if you lose, and you will every now and then keep in mind if you play long and hard enough, it must be fun or it isn't worth it.

Success is living life in fulfillment and money can't buy that! I know lots of people that have millions of dollars and are very empty, I know plenty of people that live from paycheck to pawnshop and are the happiest people I know. Money doesn't define success, if you focus on your passion and love what you do that is where you will find fulfillment.

Wealth Creation Secret No. 7.

You Must Have Patience.

The greatest business asset you can have is patience, although sometimes I have challenges with this one… lol. You must wait for the right time to make your move, if you are in the right place at the wrong time you will have pain. You must learn to adapt to your environment and act accordingly.

Learn to trust yourself, do what you do best and let your business grow naturally, pay attention and recognize opportunity. Don't procrastinate when opportunity knocks answer the door.

Wealth Creation Secret No. 8.

You must Challenge yourself, one way is to diversify your time and assets.

When you accomplish your outcome, you will find the need to be challenged once again. One way to fulfill this need is to seek out other ventures to grow and contribute.

I like the three bucket game

My first bucket I have a SNF (sleep at night factor) or some people might call it a security bucket. This bucket has 40% of my investment money in it in the form of CD's, Money Market, etc.

My second bucket is my growth bucket. This bucket has 60% of my investment money in it in the form of real estate, buy and hold, etc. this is my momentum or high return which is a little more of a risk.

My third bucket is my dream bucket or my play money. How this works is that every time the other buckets show a profit I take 10% of the profits and give it to tithes, another 10% goes into the dream bucket, 30% goes into the growth bucket and 50% goes into the SNF bucket. If I want something I must wait until my dream bucket has enough for me to buy it with.

Now to diversify my time I love to ride my bicycle in events all over the world so that takes care of that need and I am living my dream with this formula. Now you have the formula, what is your dream?

Easy and Effortless
MILLIONAIRE MONEY *secrets*
*Take control of your money, increase savings, and...
have more money for the things you really want TODAY!*

8 SECRETS ALL MILLIONAIRES HAVE IN COMMON

One of the quickest ways to build wealth is to learn from those who have achieved great wealth and mirror them.

Decide, you must first make a decision to be resolved in your commitment. To decide is to cut off, to sever, leaving no other option or alternative.

"Then indecision brings its own delays, and days are lost lamenting over lost days. Are you in earnest? Seize this very minute; what you can do, or dream you can do, begin it; Boldness has genius, power and magic in it." ~Goethe

1. Make certain it is YOUR Dream

I know I will do far more for others than myself, do you know anyone like that? Maybe even you? More often in our lives we spend more time on someone else's goals than our personal internal passionate desire. Make sure it's your passion to succeed in whatever course you chart, make certain it's your commitment to succeed in life! You define what success is, choose and be happy.

2. Do Not Call It a Goal

Mark 11:24 Therefore I tell you, whatever you ask for in prayer, believe that you have received it, and it will be yours.

Referencing the book What They Don't Teach You in the Harvard Business School, Mark McCormack shares a study conducted on students in the 1979 Harvard MBA program. In that year, the students were asked, "Have you set clear, written goals for your future and made plans to accomplish them?" Only three percent of the graduates had written goals and plans; 13 percent had goals, but they were not in writing; and a whopping 84 percent had no specific goals at all, NONE.

Ten years later, the members of the class were interviewed again, and the findings, while somewhat predictable, were nonetheless mind boggling. The 13 percent of the class who had goals were earning, on average, twice as much as the 84 percent who had no goals at all. And what about the three percent who had clear, concise written goals? They were earning, on average, ten times as much as the other 97 percent put together.

Even with the evidence of this proven method of success, most people don't have clear, measurable, time-scheduled goals written down that they work toward. Write it down with a pen and paper while in a state of anticipated expectancy. Emotion is motion.

Amazing Insight? There's more keep reading......

3. Clearly Identify Your Commitment

Begin to see your future in the present, feel it with fervent passion, see it crystal clear, this is what it takes to achieve your outcome. Clarity is

Mark 11:24 Therefore I tell you, whatever you ask for in prayer, believe that you have received it, and it will be yours.

Power! To Quote Tony Robbins ""If you talk about it, it's a dream. If you envision it, it's possible. But if you schedule it, it's real."

4. Use The Tools Around You

We must begin to use the tools around us; whether they are positive or negative motivators you must have someone in your life that is holding you accountable to reaching and achieving your goals. More often than not the negative motivators are the most compelling as I know from experience, I moved more mountains to prove to myself that I could do anything against all odds and because of the people who didn't believe in me.

Example: A Negative motivator is someone who has told you "You will never succeed". Or maybe they laughed at you when you said you're going to quit your job to begin your own business. I had many versions of this happen to me over my lifetime and it moves me every time. Thank you to all of those who didn't believe in me, I am sincerely grateful.

Write this person's name down as if you are writing a thank you card and say I am so grateful for that I_____ (whatever your outcome is) in the present tense on an index card, sticky notes, etc., and post them on your wall, in front of your computer, your cubicle, your vehicle, your locker if you have one where ever you are. So when times are tough, you look at that card and it will motivate you to keep on keeping on until you are there. The most important part of this is to celebrate as if it is already real with all of the energy and

Mark 11:24 Therefore I tell you, whatever you ask for in prayer, believe that you have received it, and it will be yours.

enthusiasm of a child.

Passion is knowing that those who pushed me forward will soon be behind me, and what I mean by that is those who didn't believe in me will soon be my strongest supporters. There are equal positives to every negative in everything.

5. Know Your Outcome and Plan it.

*WHAT is it you want? What is your outcome? What will you sacrifice to get it? *WHERE will you be? *WHEN will you accomplish it? What month, what date, what year?

*WHY do you want this? What is the consequence if you do not accomplish this? *WHO's help do you need? Who will help you? Who will you reach out to? *HOW will you make this happen? How will you get the help you need?

In your Life plan, you need to outline each of these specific characteristics of identifying at a very crystal clear level the entire process. Remember, Clarity is power!

6. Review, Plan and commit On a Daily Basis

20 Minutes every day, you need to review and re-read and note your progress on this "LIFE PLAN".

If you do not have 20 minutes, that is a complete lie. There is a special reading place we all have where we spend 15-20 minutes sometimes sitting down at. Make every should a Must. Don't just should all over yourself...

Mark 11:24 Therefore I tell you, whatever you ask for in prayer, believe that you have received it, and it will be yours.

7. Tell your Self You have Succeeded, speak your gratitude for your outcome in the present tense. Live in the gratitude of your success now, what you can do, or dream you can do you must begin it; Boldness has genius, power and magic in it.

"The size of your success is determined by the size of your belief and the fervency of your passion" Emotion is Motion.

Pay attention to your sub-conscious thoughts every single day, you must guard the doorway to your mind and allow only positive thoughts to enter. Observe how you communicate with others about your business, and where you stand as a networker. Always speak with positive verbiage to convey your message in every arena of your life.

8. Share with Others Your Conviction and Certainty of your Commitment.

Go out and share with the world about your outcome and where you are headed. Don't sit back and try to keep it a secret. Have people laugh at you, then write their name down on a card and stick on your wall!

Envision The Results and make them bigger and brighter than you ever thought possible now be grateful for the fruition.

Three Bonus Billionaire Strategies

9. The Power of Envisioning, the left brain Heart activation. Here is a proven fact, the story of Michael Jordan. Bill Bartmann was about to buy the Chicago Bulls and spent some time with the team. At that time he was writing a book

and had asked Michael about ENVISIONING... If you guys remember Michael Jordan shot a free throw with his eyes closed in the 1997 championship against the Sonics.

He was able to do that he told bill, because he envisioned it every single day!

How much time are you spending per day envisioning your success? Your dream? Your lifestyle?...

10. START

We are the only ones who can create the process of becoming wealthy. You are the only voice that can move you to want to create the freedom you desire, but most importantly you must decide and take immediate action.

Start today, start now and see how things will change for you!

11. Follow through and follow up, Often it is just one more action that creates an exponential wealth.

"MENTORING QUESTIONS TO ASK YOURSELF IN EVERY DECISION"

1) What am I doing today to get what I want?

2) Will this behavior improve my situation and move me towards what I want?... or am I settling?

3) How would the person I want to be do the thing I am about to do?

4) Who do I have to become to attract the success I want?

5) Am I willing to accept the consequences of not changing.

6) Who is in control?

7) Am I practicing to improve or doing just enough to get by?

8) What don't I SEE?

9) If my Board of Directors could see my level of effort, focus and intensity, would I get a raise or get fired?

10) Am I willing to do whatever it takes?

Mark 11:24 Therefore I tell you, whatever you ask for in prayer, believe that you have received it, and it will be yours.

Five to Thrive, 5 Steps to Financial Freedom

1. Break Free From Debt

If you carry credit card balances, debt is your biggest financial oppressor. "You're in bondage of things you bought or did in the past that you're still paying for today," says Lynnette Khalfani, author of 'Zero Debt: The Ultimate Guide to Financial Freedom' (Advantage World Press). "And it's costing you for tomorrow, because you don't have the opportunity to save or invest for your other financial goals." … … … The best strategy for paying off your debt is simple: Focus on paying off the card with the highest interest rate first, and never settle for making only the minimum payments. (You say you can't possibly squeeze any more dollars out of your budget? visit www.smartmoney.com/spending/deals/save-300-a-month-19398/ for tips on how to save $300 a month.) …

Consider this: A $5,000 balance on an 18% credit card would take nearly four years to pay off if you made a $150 monthly payment -- and would cost you $2,013 in interest. With $450 monthly payments, you'd wipe away your debt within 13 months and pay only $519 in interest. (To see how much interest your plastic will cost you, visit www.smartmoney.com/personal-finance/debt...-will-you-pay-9660/.)

Mark 11:24 Therefore I tell you, whatever you ask for in prayer, believe that you have received it, and it will be yours.

For more on beating credit card debt, and for more debt advice, We will be gearing up the toughest economic experts to help you in these times of tremendous opportunity.

2. Build a Nest Egg, Always have Cash

A cash cushion -- enough to cover three- to six-months' worth of living expenses -- is your protection against falling into debt. "Without it, any time an emergency comes up you're forced to resort to plastic," Khalfani says.

The good news: Thanks to rising interest rates your cash can earn decent returns in the bank. Visit www.smartmoney.com/spending/deals/5ive-t...ng-interest-rates-0/ for the best deals.

3. Fortify your assets

According to the Consumer Bankruptcy Project, the major reasons for bankruptcy filings are job loss and medical problems.

The best way to protect yourself: Make sure you have adequate insurance. "Most people are woefully underinsured," Khalfani says. "The problem is, if you suffer any kind of setback, illness or disability and don't have enough insurance to cover that, you're thrown into financial crisis."

If you aren't offered health insurance through your job, consider private health insurance. Visit www.smartmoney.com/spending/deals/buying...lth-insurance-14819/ for advice on finding the most affordable policy with the best coverage.

Disability insurance is another tricky area. Most

Mark 11:24 Therefore I tell you, whatever you ask for in prayer, believe that you have received it, and it will be yours.

employers offer it, but for many people, the policies don't provide adequate coverage.

Contact me if you need a worksheet to help you figure out where you are at and how to get where you are going.

4. Creat a budget

Your mortgage payments, insurance and food -- the so-called "must-haves" -- should comprise no more than 50% of your monthly spending. Then, allocate a solid 20% to savings for retirement, college costs and other long-term savings goals. Finally, leave a pleasing 30% for the fun stuff, be it golfing or clubbing, buying shoes or fine dining.

Need help creating a budget? email me lisa@drlisacoaching.com

5. Master your emotions, Create Peace of Mind!

It's a subject no one likes to discuss, but the fact is that having a will is more important than you may think. "People have big misconceptions about why and who should create a will," Khalfani says. "A big one is that wills are only for people with big estates, elderly people, people who are married or have kids. All of those are myths."

Even if you're a recent college grad renting a studio apartment with two roommates a will is always a good idea. Once you start building a portfolio and acquiring assets, When the time has come to draw up a will, you have already done so. Hiring a lawyer may cost anywhere between $500 and $1,000, depending on where you live and the complexity of the paperwork. But at online law clinics like Buildawill.com and

Legalzoom.com a basic will costs as little as $19.95 and $69, respectively.

Also, consider a VUL (Variable Universal Life), it is never to soon or to late to start also a ROTH IRA is a great place to start, it is especially a good idea for people nearing retirement. The VUL is a better vehicle when you are planning on buying life insurance.

Feel free to contact me at lisa@drlisacoaching.com or visit http://www.drlisacoaching.com/index.php?option=com_kunena&Itemid=136&func=view&catid=5&id=11

Life Will Give You What You Ask Of It

Great players and great teams are willing to work hard. Average players and average teams want it easy.

Higgins vs. Lyle- Golf I have a friend, who is still a good golfer at age 65, who always regretted that he didn't try out for the golf team in college. His excuses were that he was from a small town of 2000 people and the local golf course was only 9 holes with sand greens. My friend went to the most prestigious and largest University in the state. He felt that coming from the small town that his high school education was inferior to that of the students from large cities and that he would have to outwork these students in order to achieve success in college and life, thus might not have time to devote to golf and make the golf team. He also worried that his golf course was inferior to those golfers coming from country clubs, taking lessons from professionals and playing tournaments in the summer. He later became friends with someone on the golf team who was a 2-time college all American. There was no question that the all American was a better player than my friend who made a telling remark to me. He said that when they played together that if he(my friend) got 1 or 2 under par during the round that he would become "protective" and try to make pars and save his round and keep it right around par for the total round. Whereas his friend if he was 2 or 3 under par after 5 holes he would want to know what the course record was. In other words he became even more aggressive, while my friend became more conservative. In Hind sight, my friend knows that if he would have gone to a smaller school, he wouldn't have worried about his ability to do well in school and is confident he could have made the golf team. While he is proud of his degree from the more prestigious University, he has always regretted not trying to make

Mark 11:24 Therefore I tell you, whatever you ask for in prayer, believe that you have received it, and it will be yours.

the golf team. The morale of this story is that there are different goals or levels of success in life. My friend went on to have a successful career in banking, but never quite got to where he maybe should have gotten to; i.e. the president or a senior level of management in the bank. His friend on the other hand, had a good golf career, playing in 2 U.S Opens and 2 British Opens, but lacked the "mental edge" needed to become a household name in the world of golf. My take on this is that there are many variables in the race for success. One must decide and set goals for where they want to go. I don't think it matters what size town you grew up in, what school you went to, or what kind of golf course you started on. There are numerous stories of great success in politics, business, and life that have grown up in these environments. The old saying is "it's not the size of the dog in the fight, but the size of fight in the dog that counts." So, by being aggressive isn't the only answer. You can be too aggressive, hit the ball out of bounds and into the lake, make a triple bogie, and instead of being 3 under par, you are now 1 over par. In life, by being over aggressive in your job, you have exceeded your authority to lend or to purchase or whatever by 30% because you just knew that it was a great deal and would make your company lots more money; A good example of this would be in 2006 when the real estate market was a feeding frenzy and then suddenly fell in 2007 and progressively continued to spiral down. So now, you get fired or at least demoted with more supervision, restrictions, ect. One way to avoid this trap is by having a mentor, but it doesn't have to be someone in your company. It may be someone close to the top of the ladder or a rising young star who is only a couple of levels above you. It's obvious that you don't want to be so closely tied to that individual that if his star burns out that you crash with him or her. This choice is very important, kind of like choosing your life partner. You should be able to talk to your mentor about trivial things as well as important things. Remember that his or her time is not limitless, so pick your spots and don't become a burden.

Another golf story from my banker friend. His golfing ability was an asset to his career. He said that every interview he went to he ultimately got the subject around to golf and his 2 handicap was a big plus. Of course all jobs don't involve entertaining and building customer relationships like banking. The story is that at the bank employee's annual golf tournament the bright rising star way oversold his golf ability to get paired with the Chairman of The Board. Needless to say, his status went downhill when he shot a 140, let loose several four letter words, and drank too many beers. Your job and your reputation are 24 hour days. Your social life, your hobbies, ect. as they all get interwoven into your career. It's not a big plus, but to get picked up for a DWI after leaving the strip club like the friend of Mr. Lyle, it should be a given, and also the actions of your spouse and even your children can have a major impact on your career. It takes such a small act of kindness to enhance your career like simply being nice to people you work with. It takes such a small amount of your most valuable commodity, time, to speak to the security guard you see every morning instead of passing by without even looking at him or her. Sure he/she probably doesn't advise the CEO as to who gets promoted, but just maybe his neighbor or cousin becomes your best customer or the lawsuit you win as his attorney because of the security guards recommendation. To me, it's very obvious to succeed in life and your career that you have to work hard and make some sacrifices. Sure some people take shortcuts and cheat and get away with it, but the odds are against you. Never be ashamed to ask for help. There are

Mark 11:24 Therefore I tell you, whatever you ask for in prayer, believe that you have received it, and it will be yours.

people who have thought about and done the thing or project you are involved with. To follow up on the earlier mention of being nice to people, also praise those that helped you complete projects and goals. A little praise goes a long ways. Be a team player. I saw a quote recently I liked "Great players and great teams are willing to work hard, while average players and average teams want it easy." In summary, the old saying "you have to play the cards you are dealt" is true, but not really. We don't control who our parents are, our environment we grow up in, but we can control how much effort we put into our education, be it a Jr. college or Harvard. We can control our progression after our former education learning by always striving to learn more be it by reading some of the many great "self-help" books available learning from those we work with, those we network with, our mentor, and our experiences. If you ever get to the point where you are not striving to learn more or better yourself you are in deep do-do. Always remember one thing, we cannot control others nor can we control life circumstances but we can control how we respond. We can choose to be the author of our own lives and every day we get a new opportunity to make new choices. Choose and be happy.

Mark 11:24 Therefore I tell you, whatever you ask for in prayer, believe that you have received it, and it will be yours.

Think Before You Invest

Something to think about before you invest, I have a friend who is a retired Investment Advisor; he once gave his opinion to people on investments. Since he is retired and not trying to sell you or anybody else anything, I asked for him to share his investment philosophy.

The two main things I would emphasize are that not one size fits all and that you need to be proactive because you have greater interest in you than anyone else ever will. Everyone's circumstances are different, i.e., your family, their current needs, their future needs after you are gone. Are you likely to inherit assets at some point, do you need extra dollars for your retirement, are you building toward your retirement, and so on. So, it stands to reason that while growth stocks might be good for some, others may need income producing assets. Also, one's risk tolerance is critical, not all of us are as willing to assume risk as a reward for a greater return.

To help you with that criteria and advice toward making those important decisions, it stands to reason that you need good professional advice from CPA's, tax attorneys, and investment advisors. Most of us have the goal of leaving as much as possible to our spouse, children, charity, etc., so estate planning dovetails into investment advice. I, like most of us, look for bargain, but here it often times is wise to pay a little bit more for good advice, rather than cheap advice.

Mark 11:24 Therefore I tell you, whatever you ask for in prayer, believe that you have received it, and it will be yours.

The other important point that I would make is that our government, both federal and state (also some cities) are trying to get as much of your money as they possibly can. Everything you buy is taxed (sales tax, real estate tax, personal property tax, estate tax). Most states have personal income tax, so in addition to federal tax, you pay your state for interest earned, dividends received, and capital gains tax, another reason for advice.

If you have great new wealth, maybe from an inheritance, or as some people I know who think they are going to become wealthy from a certain currency swap, don't flaunt your wealth. Keep a low profile. You are a great target for scam artists, also for trial or tort lawyers. There are some books and services that can help you if you are in or anticipate being in these circumstances. If you have new money or are beginning retirement, perhaps you should change your life style to a calmer existence. You will enjoy life more and live longer.

Do good things with your money, i.e. charity. Do it on a consistent basis, follow your heart and always remember that giving is living. Pray for guidance, but please don't force your belief, as this can override your mindset to where you won't recognize happiness when you see it. Be friendly, not someone who is critical of other's lifestyle, or views. We are all free and entitled to our own opinions.

Mark 11:24 Therefore I tell you, whatever you ask for in prayer, believe that you have received it, and it will be yours.

A great quote, from George Santayana, "Those who forget the past are condemned to repeat it." Over the years, we all make mistakes; those who remember the past hopefully avoid making the same mistakes over and over, notice what's not working and change your approach, notice what is working and keep doing it, learn to recognize the difference. Above all THINK, each move or investment that you make should be a chess game, think 5 moves ahead, know your outcome and act with the end in mind. A survey found that 3% think; 12% think they think; the rest muddle thru life and fail to achieve their investment goals or life goals. May God bless you, but remember to THINK things thru and get GOOD ADVICE.

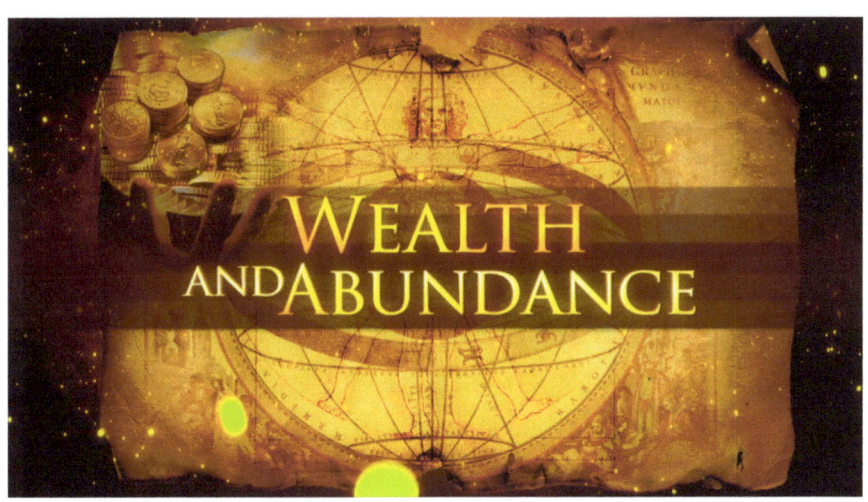

The Power Of Mastery

Mastery in one's career and self growth simply requires that we consistently and constantly produce results beyond the ordinary into the extraordinary by producing outstanding results. Mastery is attained by consistently stepping outside of our comfort zone, going beyond our limits with the knowledge that the only limits there are in life are the ones we set for ourselves. Open your eyes, listen to hear, feel your achievement and breakthrough your limits to the success you deserve. For most people, this starts with technical excellence in a chosen field and a commitment to that excellence. This needs to begin with a clear vision and the decision to do what it takes making success your only option. If you are willing to commit yourself to excellence, to surround yourself with things that represent excellence, your life will change because you are your five closest friends. (When we speak of miracles, we speak of events or experiences that go beyond the ordinary into the extraordinary.)

Mark 11:24 Therefore I tell you, whatever you ask for in prayer, believe that you have received it, and it will be yours.

It's remarkable how much mediocrity we live with, surrounding ourselves with daily reminders that the average is the acceptable, we must decide this behavior of mediocrity is UNACCEPTABLE. More often than not you will find the common belief is limited thinking with a mindset of go to school to get a good job to retire comfortable and then you die. I urge you to look inside yourself and identify the things that are keeping you powerless to go beyond any "limit" that you have arbitrarily set for yourself, take a moment to assess all of these things around you that promote your being "average", now take action to remove these things from your life even if this means making new friends, because often your friends will bring guilt to your dreams by saying "oh, you think you are better than me?" or "what makes you think you can do that?" these are dream thieves and you need dream achievers in your circle of friends, with that being said you must reach up to those that frighten you and cultivate friendships where you once thought were impossible you will be surprised how many will be excited to mentor you. To begin mastery is to remove everything in your environment that represents mediocrity, removing those things that are limiting. Again, one way is to surround yourself with friends who ask more of themselves than anyone else ever would because these are the ones who step up to defy the odds, to set new standards and to be the change they want to see in this world by being the example. It is this recipe for success that you must emulate to achieve your success because if you find someone who is successfully doing what you are passionate about you simply have to follow their formula to achieve the same result.

Mark 11:24 Therefore I tell you, whatever you ask for in prayer, believe that you have received it, and it will be yours.

Another step on the path to mastery is the removal of resentment toward masters whether on your level, below or above your level, this action is very important because these are your potential mentors. We are always learning from each other so respect is critical, if you don't respect the person please respect their gifts to contribute to others even if you don't agree. Develop humility so that while in the presence of masters you are emotionally available with an open heart and an open mind to grow from the experience. Do not compare yourself to others and do not resent people who have mastery, remain open, respectful and receptive; allow the experience to enrich you like the planting of a seed within you that, with nourishment, will grow into your own individual unique mastery.

We are all created equal, mastery is learned through education, life experiences and the examples laid before us. A true master will embrace their flaws and weaknesses as a tool to relate to others with a genuine appreciation of their circumstances. A master recognizes this fault as a foundation for building the extraordinary instead of using it as an excuse for inactivity, use this as a vehicle for growing, which is essential in the process of attaining mastery. You must be able to learn, grow and accept criticism without condemning yourself to accept results and improve upon them. Growth is essential to power and mastery because if you are not growing you are dying.

Success Without Fulfillment is Failure

We give words meaning, we define what success is, and we create our own destiny based on our own internal blueprint.

Mark 11:24 Therefore I tell you, whatever you ask for in prayer, believe that you have received it, and it will be yours.

Today, people feel a lot of unnecessary and unneeded stress caused by comparing themselves to others. This stress puts a toll on both their mental and physical health. In fact, even the CDC says that "emotional health" can be up to 85% responsible for physical health.

First, you must understand that your physical surroundings determine who you "hang" with and who you "hang" with is a large determinant of your self-worth. You are a reflection of your five closest friends. This is because we as social creatures tend to base our opinions of ourselves on comparisons between ourselves and those in our immediate circles. This can work both for you and against you. Surrounding yourself with others who have achieved things – and a level of success – you desire to achieve, gives you examples after which to model your behavior. On the other hand, if you are constantly comparing yourselves to these people, that can cause you immense stress. Thus, this is a highly individualized matter that you must consider on a personal level and how these comparisons affect you in particular.

Some people need to be "reaching up" to be motivated. While others need to excel within their personal group to feel confident enough to eventually reach up. It is a fine balance. That is why we will be examining this subject over the next couple of weeks from both angles but we'll hit on a quick summary now...

If you are one who gets stressed by comparing yourself to your more successful friends, neighbors, or co-workers, one of the quickest ways to change any negative feelings, jealousy, or status envy you might have is to ensure you also have people who are at your current socio-economic and enviro-economic status in your circle as well.

Mark 11:24 Therefore I tell you, whatever you ask for in prayer, believe that you have received it, and it will be yours.

This idea was put forth in "How to Get Over Status Anxiety" at www.psychologytoday.com. This is not to imply that you necessarily change your circle of friends. It's just that you need to be more conscientious of who you compare yourself to on a regular basis.

For example, you can seek out those you can better and more appropriate identify with through social and civic groups. And sometimes, one can better flourish by seeking out "smaller settings" in which to work and play as well. Sometimes successes are easier to come by and recognize in such a setting. You must also learn to recognize your own successes – in their own right – and use them to balance what you feel are you failures or shortcomings that only exist in comparison to others. Especially comparisons to others who might have more advantages – or resources – than you do at your disposal.

Perhaps most importantly, learn to use this "envy" for good. Use it to propel you to greater heights. Instead of thinking, "Poor me. I don't have..." or "I'll never be able to do what so-and-so did because I didn't grow up rich" or "I'm not as educated so I am not as smart as...", and letting those things get you down on yourself, begin to consider how your particular circumstances served you. Only you havethe power to decide that. Has a lack of certain things in your life forced you to be resourceful? Has your lack of money in your life put you in a position to empathize with those facing certain problems that only you – with your underprivileged or even middle-class background – can really understand? Maybe your lack of formal education has driven you to really study the world – or independently – so that you actually have more practical knowledge than your more "classroom educated" counterparts?

Mark 11:24 Therefore I tell you, whatever you ask for in prayer, believe that you have received it, and it will be yours.

On the other hand, if you are someone who needs to be consistently challenged to strive for "more", then add people to your circle of influence who are currently where you desire to be and mirror them. This will take years off your journey to success and allow you to arrive at your destination in a much shorter time. There are always two sides to every coin and while some need to remain secure in their current situation – and there is nothing wrong with that if that is what gives you greater emotional security and satisfaction – I, on the other hand, am always searching for growth.

I believe that wherever you are at some point in time, you have made an "appointment" to be there. Being "wealthy" isn't just a question of how much money you have, but rather having what you want. It has been said by many that success without fulfillment is failure. Wealth isn't absolute, it's relative to desire... SELF ESTEEM= success divided by expectation. Meaning, people base their self-worth on their definition of success. To be successful, one must be prepared for opportunity and then answer the door when it knocks – or lower your expectation – either way decide what works for you.

For today, the key here is remembering that everything in life serves you equally. Aside from the other practical steps mentioned above, your attitude – and view – on these things, can change your life as much as (or more!) than anything. For the next few weeks, we will cover this more intricately. In the meantime, remember that success – for you – is merely a matter of how you define it. What is your definition of "success"?

 Retirement is the waiting room for expirement so let us talk about last things first... Are you laying up treasures in heaven or building mansions below, will you be among the chosen of God or with the foolish ones who say I will tear down the barns and build greater? I will say to my soul "I think I will retire" then comes the call of God from glory, tonight your soul is required of thee so where are your treasures? One day you are going to die and then what will be your strength? God doesn't say not to be rich, God wants us to prosper, he also wants us to realize what the true eternal investment is... So when your thinking about investing make certain your first investment is one that will carry you into eternity, I am not talking about tithing I am talking about the salvation of your soul... We cannot take anything with us so to lay an investment in eternity through Christ will payoff exponentially, investments made in the name of any other will result in eternal loss. So first things first, now that we have talked about your investment in experiment we will now talk about your investment in retirement... ~Dr. Lisa Christiansen

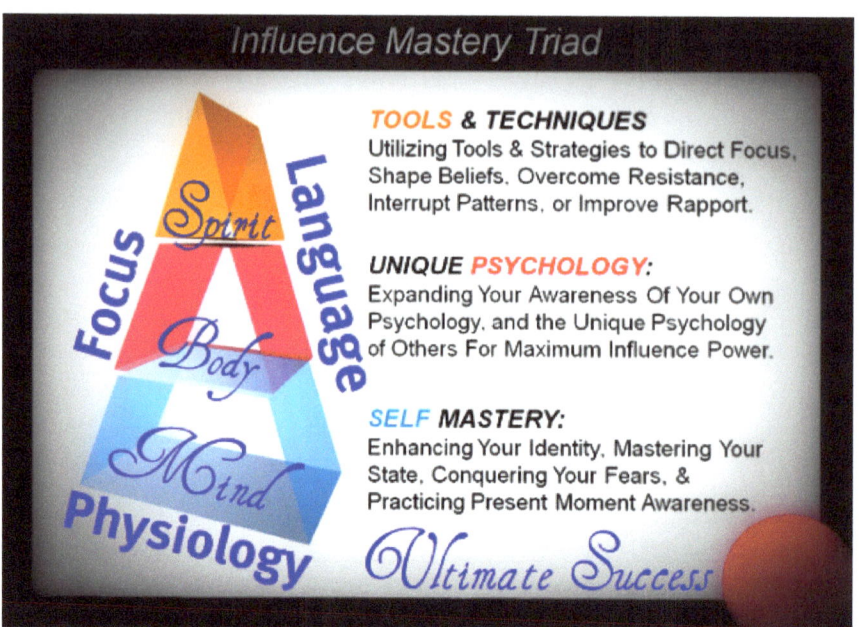

Your Success Blueprint

11 Strategies To Reprogram Your Blueprint

SUCCESS BLUEPRINT #1

Confidence, Self-esteem and Self-image

The key to confidence is acquiescing a heightened level of positive self-esteem by believing that you are intelligent enough, good enough, and deserving to succeed your desired results.

Ask yourself "who do I need to become to achieve the life I am committed to living?"

When you mirror the self-image of a person who easily does what you desire to do this action will almost guarantee that you will achieve your outcome.

Mark 11:24 Therefore I tell you, whatever you ask for in prayer, believe that you have received it, and it will be yours.

SUCCESS BLUEPRINT #2

Driven By Your Purpose - Your Why

It is not enough to be motivated to reach your outcome; you must be driven by your why. Your shoulds become musts and you must decide to live on purpose, show up for your dreams with a compelling reason. It is impossible to be this driven unless you are being pushed by something more than just surviving, you must have a passion so intense that it consumes you from the core of who you are.

You must be motivated from within and maintain momentum through ups and downs, it's critical to constantly focus on your purpose, why you want the outcome must be the fundamental focus with every decision. A weak purpose means failure 99.999% of the time.

SUCCESS BLUEPRINT #3

What You Focus On Is What You Get

Your brain does not know the difference between fact or fiction and equally your brain will not make you a liar. Visualize your outcome in the present with clarity because Clarity is power. When you visualize what you want with intense emotion your psychology will control your physiology and in turn control your environment.

Just as a dream can seem so real, you have the ability to bring it to fruition by visualizing your desire with

Mark 11:24 Therefore I tell you, whatever you ask for in prayer, believe that you have received it, and it will be yours.

belief, when you live your dream in the present in your subconscious your mind will continually move you in the direction to make it happen. Everything that was ever accomplished by anyone was first seen in the mind's eye. It is no different for you because you have the ability to live life on your terms. When you see it as real, accomplished, as done, as a storming success in your mind, then you will bring it to fruition.

SUCCESS BLUEPRINT #4

Tenacity

The will to succeed can overcome every limitation no matter what your challenge is. The only limitations are the ones we set for ourselves, get out of your own way.

SUCCESS BLUEPRINT #5

Decide

Once you make a decision you will succeed because to decide is to cut off, to sever, bringing success is the only option.

"Yes, I Can," will become your new mantra.

And as your self-confidence grows, your stress levels will plummet and your willingness to take action will soar.

SUCCESS BLUEPRINT #6

Follow Up With A Plan

You must know exactly what you need to do to reach a outcome or make a change in yourself is vital. Inconsistent actions lead to failure. It is essential to follow through on whatever actions are required of you each and every day. Review your why every day in every decision and ask your self "is what I am about to do getting me closer to my outcome?"

Before you reach your outcomes have new ones in place to continue the momentum of your growth, keep a vision board or journal and cross of each accomplishment as you move forward in your victories. Your thoughts are what create your life. If you simply do what little is required of you each day, you'll get to your desired outcome. Just like the other people who always get what they want in life.

SUCCESS BLUEPRINT #7

Enjoy The Journey

Anything worth having is a challenge, if it were easy everyone would do it, you are extraordinary because you are willing to set new standards and defy the odds. Is the activity of accomplishing a challenging outcome always fun? No. If it were fun, everyone would be taking action? Wouldn't you look forward to the next challenge? Wouldn't you experience your mistakes, setbacks, delays, and criticism differently than you do now? Yes, you would. Instill in your mind an alert

Mark 11:24 Therefore I tell you, whatever you ask for in prayer, believe that you have received it, and it will be yours.

awareness of the fun and satisfaction you can have all along the path toward reaching your desired outcome. For example, in areas where you don't now enjoy the tasks, like exercising, with the statements steering your consciousness toward a love for all things physical, you'll easily see the activities as enjoyable, or at least gain a greater appreciation for the tasks just like the millions who see it that way already. Discover new ways to make it more pleasant. You'll look at the situation in whatever way you need to see it so that you feel good instead of depressed over your fate of having to do this set of tasks or activities related to your outcome.

Your stress levels will go down considerably and you should be able to reach your outcome easier than you could ever have imagined just a short time ago.

SUCCESS BLUEPRINT #8

Be Teachable And Trainable

Duplication is the key. The most important outcomes in our lives often don't fall within our natural abilities and current level of knowledge. We usually need to do some research, explore options and learn new ideas, techniques, facts, skills, or principles. The problem is, most people don't want to be bothered to learn anything new. It's viewed as too much work, as boring or unpleasant, or cuts into relaxation and recreation time. You need to be ready and willing to learn what you must to reach your outcome and love doing it.

SUCCESS BLUEPRINT #9

See Things Better Than They Are

Whatever your outcome is, the truest test of how you are progressing toward it lies not in how you function when you are moving along smoothly, but in how you act and react when problems are presented to you. Bad decisions, mistakes and setbacks are simply part of the process to get where you want to go, and absolutely no reason to quit, to get upset, or even slow your progress. So whether you're trying to gain a habit, lose a habit, reach success in business or relationships, or overcome depression or anxiety, flood your mind with self-instructions telling yourself that you are optimistic and level-headed through your setbacks and moments of challenge. With conditioning, your desire and determination will grow and stay high even after bigger, more serious setbacks. You'll become one of those people that always knows or figures out what to do and makes sure it gets done without delay.

SUCCESS BLUEPRINT #10

Appreciation

One of the biggest frustrations most people experience is to experience success in reaching a big outcome or status level only to see it all go away. To watch yourself stop doing what you did to reach your success in the first place. The strong tendency is to forget what it took to succeed. This is why people who have been good at something for years can make mistakes and correct them fairly rapidly. People who are just gaining a skill, attitude, or habit can very easily mess up once and quit, or they can fall back into old routines without even knowing it. When changes are desired, conditioning is critical. One of the things you MUST do to make your changes stick is to pay attention and appreciate what it took to get there, to enjoy the end result, to enjoy the rewards, to acknowledge your success and efforts so that when temptations arise you can understand how you came to succeed. This way, you'll keep your new ways and continue to succeed when 19 out of 20 are failing, predictably going back to old ways of thinking and acting within days, weeks, or months.

SUCCESS BLUEPRINT #11

Gratitude

Most people who reach some long-term outcome or who quit some bad habit self sabotage after they worked hard to reach their outcome. They don't see in their own mind that they have accomplished anything. When you accomplish anything, whether it is large or small, give yourself a boost by rewarding yourself for it. Accept other's praise for what you have accomplished. It's time to give yourself and accept from others the credit you deserve.

Mark 11:24 Therefore I tell you, whatever you ask for in prayer, believe that you have received it, and it will be yours.

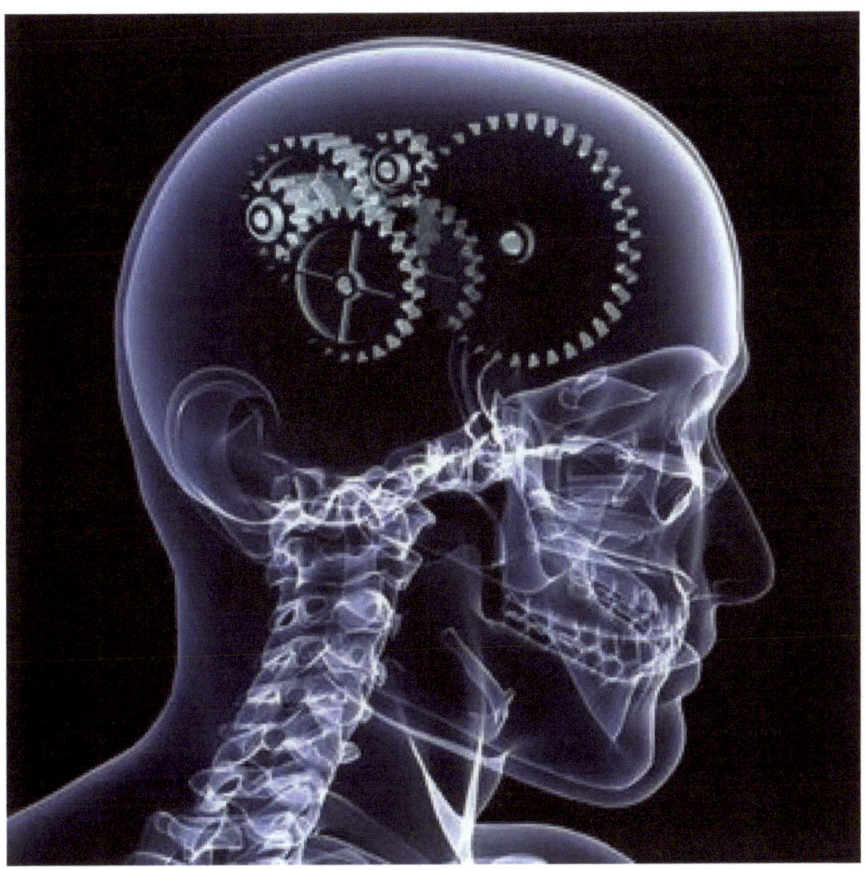

Millionaire Blueprint

Lisa Christiansen

Millionaires have more in common than their bank accounts, for self-made millionaires, achieving success took courage, the art of influence, vision and passion. Here are the most common strategies to the seven-figure bank account and what you can do to sharpen some of these skills to find your missing money link and live life on your terms.

Mark 11:24 Therefore I tell you, whatever you ask for in prayer, believe that you have received it, and it will be yours.

1. Create Independent Thinking

Millionaires think different; they are often referred to as the crazy ones, the misfits, the rebels, the troublemakers, the round pegs in the square holes, the ones who see things differently, they're not fond of rules, and they have no respect for the status quo. You can quote them, disagree with them, glorify and vilify them, about the only thing you can't do is ignore them because they change things. They push the human race forward, and while some may see them as crazy, we see genius, because the people who are crazy enough to think they can change the world, are the ones who do. They think different not just about money, about everything. We all have the same 24 hours in a day, the time and energy everybody else spends conforming, millionaires make time to create their own destiny by cutting their own path. Since thoughts impact actions, people who want to be wealthy should think in a way that will get them to that goal by recognizing that a goal is a dream and an outcome is scheduled. Independent means digging deep in your subconscious to take control at the core level and having the courage to step into the unknown for what is important to you. In life you will find two things... a way and an excuse. For what you want enough you will find a way, For what you don't you will find an excuse... Those most successful in life are the ones brave enough to step out into the unknown So, the lesson here is to forge your own way, and let your success drive you to learn the art of making your money work for you instead of you working for your money. Just look at Bill Gates, A self-made millionaire after dropping out of Harvard to pursue his vision. Although he didn't take what many assume to be the usual path to success, his ability to ask a better question to get a better answer has been his blueprint to success.

Mark 11:24 Therefore I tell you, whatever you ask for in prayer, believe that you have received it, and it will be yours.

2. Become A Visionary

Millionaires are creative visionaries with a positive attitude. In other words, wealthy people not only have big dreams, they also believe it will come true which causes them to find the most important part of this vision, their why because only 20% are the mechanics the other 80% is the compelling why that becomes their driving force. They revisit this why and approach it with a map that moves them closer in every decision everyday. As such, wealth seekers should set lofty goals and not be brave enough to step up, defy the odds and step out of your comfort zone, take the calculated risks of uncharted territories.Bill Gates, the world's richest person in 2009, did just that. The American chairman of Microsoft is one of the founding entrepreneurs who brought personal computers to the masses. Gates jumped into the personal computers business in 1975 and held on tight, creating Microsoft Windows in 1985. When consumers began to bring computers into their homes, Gates was ready to profit from this new age.

3. Sharpen Success

SkillsWriter Dennis Kimbro interviewed successful people to determine the traits they had in common for his book, "Think and Grow Rich" (1992). What he discovered is they concentrated on their area of excellence. Millionaires also partner with others to supplement their weaker skills. If you don't know what you are good at ask your friends and family. Utilize training tools and seek mentors to refine your strong skills. To insure success seek mentors who are already successful at your desired outcome and mirror their formula, you will achieve success in a fraction of the time it took them.

4. Live In Passion

It has been said most eloquently by billionaire Warren Buffett "Money is a by-product of something I like to do very much." When you enjoy what you are doing it is not a job it is your passion that you happen to profit from, a job is an acronym for Just Over Broke. People who interact with money for a living often love creating new ventures and influencing others to complete a transaction. Find your passion, statistics claim the average millionaire doesn't find it until age 45, and tends to be 54 before becoming a millionaire. Kimbro found that millionaires tried an average of 17 opportunities before they were successful. If you want to be rich, stop doing things you don't enjoy and do what you love. Have sensory acuity, notice what's working and keep moving forward and recognize what's not working and change your approach until it does work.

5. Investment

Millionaires are willing to sacrifice time and money to achieve their goals. They are willing to take a risk now for the opportunity of achieving something greater in the future. Investing using the theory of compounding is a great way to diversify your assets and the growth of your profits. Using the 3 bucket rule is my strategy, if you want to know more read my article "Wealth Creation".

6. Influence

Millionaires are constantly presenting their ideas and utilizing the art of influence to cause others to invest in them. Masters of the art are oblivious to critics and naysayers.

In other words, they don't take "no" for an answer. Millionaires also have good social skills. In fact, when writer T. Harv Eker analyzed the results of a survey of 753 millionaires for his book, "Secrets of the Millionaire Mind" (2005), he found social skills were more important than IQ. Just look at Donald Trump. His fortune has fluctuated over the years, but his ability to sell himself - whether as a TV personality or as the force behind a line of neckties - has always brought him back among the ranks of celebrity millionaires. The ability to communicate with people is essential to selling your idea. Contrary to the traditional view of salesmen, millionaires cite honesty as an important factor in their success. If you want to be a millionaire, be an honest salesman and polish your social skills.

Becoming a millionaire is not an outcome that can be achieved overnight for most people, it is for the disciplined who are willing to be unreasonable. It is achieved by making smart and often bold decisions, putting their skills to the best use possible and doggedly pursuing their vision. If you can learn anything about millionaires, it's that for many of them, their riches are not necessarily what most sets them apart from the rest of the world it is what they did to earn those millions that really stands out.

Mark 11:24 Therefore I tell you, whatever you ask for in prayer, believe that you have received it, and it will be yours.

Daily Resolutions For Highly Successful People

The Seven Habits are not a set of separate or piecemeal psyche-up formulas, they are in harmony with the natural laws of growth, they provide an incremental, sequential, highly integrated approach to the development of personal and interpersonal effectiveness. They move us progressively on a Maturity Continuum from dependence to independence to interdependence.

#1 Be Proactive

#2 Begin With The End In Mind

#3 Put First Things First

#4 Think Win/Win

#5 Seek First To Understand Then To Be Understood

#6 Synergize

#7 Sharpen The Saw

Mark 11:24 Therefore I tell you, whatever you ask for in prayer, believe that you have received it, and it will be yours.

Dependence is the paradigm of you, you take care of me, you come through for me, you didn't come through, I blame you for the results. Dependent people need others to get what they want.

Independence is the paradigm of I, I can do it, I am responsible, I am self-reliant, I can choose, Independent people can get what they want through their own effort.

Interdependence is the paradigm of we, we can do it, we can cooperate, we can combine our talents and abilities and create something greater together. Interdependent people combine their own efforts with the efforts of others to achieve their greatest success.

Effective Interdependence can only be built on a foundation of true independence.

If we want to change a situation, we first have to change ourselves and to change ourselves effectively; we first have to change our perceptions. Perception is reality... you give words and actions meaning, change your belief and you will change your future. Once you master your emotions you are in control of your destiny, conquer the mind and your body will follow. It is when you make a change in your psychology that you will create a much-needed change in your physiology.

Albert Einstein observed - " The significant problems we face cannot be solved at the same level of thinking we were at when we created them".

The way we see the problem is the problem.

Mark 11:24 Therefore I tell you, whatever you ask for in prayer, believe that you have received it, and it will be yours.

Effective People are not problem-minded they're opportunity-minded. They feed opportunities and starve problems.

Paradigms are powerful because they create the lens through which we see the world. The power of a paradigm shift is the essential power of quantum change whether that shift is an instantaneous or a slow and deliberate process.

We must look at the lens through which we see the world as well as at the world we see and understand that the lens itself shapes how we interpret the world.

We simply assume that the way we see things is the way they really are or the way they should be and our attitudes and behaviors grow out of those assumptions.

Each of us has many maps in our head - which can be divided into two main categories: maps of *the way things are*, or *realities* and maps of *the way things should be* or *values*. We interpret everything we experience through these mental maps.

Our character, basically, is a composite of our habits because they are consistent often-unconscious patterns they constantly daily express our character and produce our effectiveness … or ineffectiveness.

You are NOT your habits; you CAN replace old patterns of self-defeating behavior with new patterns, new habits of effectiveness, happiness and trust-based relationships.

Mark 11:24 Therefore I tell you, whatever you ask for in prayer, believe that you have received it, and it will be yours.

Highly Proactive People recognize their "responsability the ability to choose their response. They do not blame circumstances, conditions, or conditioning for their behavior. Their behavior is a product of their own conscious choice based on values rather than a product of their conditions based on feeling.

Reactive People focus on circumstances over which they have no control, the negative energy generated by that focus combined with neglect in areas they could do something about causes their Circle of Influence to shrink.

Proactive People focus their efforts on the things they can do something about, the nature of their energy is positive, enlarging, and magnifying causing their Circle of Influence to increase.

Whatever is at the center of our life will be the source of our security, guidance, wisdom and power.

Nine Traditional Wealth Lessons

Lesson #1: Does Income equal wealth?

While higher-income households tend to have more wealth than lower and middle-income households, the size of a paycheck explains only 30% of the variation of wealth among households. What really matters are how much of the income is invested, if you have multiple streams of income and how you choose to invest. **On average, millionaires invest nearly 20% of their income.**

Lesson #2: Should I Budget?

The majority of millionaires have a budget they are committed to. Of those who don't have an artificial economic environment of scarcity," more commonly known as "pay yourself first." In other words, they invest a good chunk of their income before they can spend any of it.

As for those who do budget and plan out their expenses for the coming year, no, they don't enjoy it any more than the rest of us. Yes, they do appreciate the "payoff," as well as fear the consequences of not doing it. **It's much easier to budget if you visualize the long-term benefits of this action.**

Lesson #3: Do I Know Where My Money Goes?

Similar to the previous point, almost two-thirds of millionaires can answer "yes" to this question: "Do you know how much your family spends each year for food, clothing, and shelter?" In contrast, only 35% of high-income non-millionaires answered yes to this question. Millionaires are more likely to track their spending.

Lesson #4: Where Do I Want My Money To Go?

Another two-thirds of millionaires answered "yes" to this question: "Do you have a clearly defined set of daily, weekly, monthly, annual, and lifetime goals?" One example: a woman who wants to have $5 million by the age of 46, at which point she offer a hand up to other entrepreneurs. At the time of this articles publication, she had already reached millionaire status on an annual income of $100,000. As for those who answered "no" to the question, many of them are retired and have already reached their goal of financial independence.

Lesson #5: Is Time Money?

All this budgeting and goal setting takes time, but millionaires are willing to make the time. **Prodigious accumulators of wealth spend nearly twice as many hours per month planning their investments as under accumulators of wealth.** The majority of PAWs agreed with the following statements, while the majority of UAWs did not:

Mark 11:24 Therefore I tell you, whatever you ask for in prayer, believe that you have received it, and it will be yours.

"I spend a lot of time planning my financial future."

"Usually, I have sufficient time to handle my investments properly."

"When it comes to the allocation of my time, I place the management of my assets before my other activities."

You don't have to earn a big six-figure salary for planning to pay off. In a survey of 854 middle-income workers, Danko and Stanley found "a strong positive correlation" between investment planning and wealth accumulation. This extra planning doesn't just happen. According to the authors, "Most PAWs have a regimented planning schedule. Each week, each month, each year, they plan their investments."

Lesson #6: Why Should I Love My Home?

Your choice of home and how often you choose a new one will determine your ability to accumulate wealth. According to *The Millionaire Next Door*, that wealthy family has been next door for quite a while. Half of millionaires have lived in the same house for more than 20 years.

In *Stop Acting Rich*, Thomas Stanley digs deeper into how your address affects your spending, writing:

Nothing has a greater impact on your wealth and your consumption than your choices of house and neighborhood. *If you live in a high-price home in an exclusive community, you will spend more than you should and your ability to save and build wealth will be compromised.... People who live in million-dollar homes are not millionaires. They may be high-income producers but, by trying to emulate glittering rich millionaires, they are living a treadmill*

Mark 11:24 Therefore I tell you, whatever you ask for in prayer, believe that you have received it, and it will be yours.

existence.

He cites several statistics to back this up, including:

Ninety percent of millionaires live in homes valued below $1 million; 28.3% live in homes valued at $300,000 or less.

On average, millionaires have a mortgage that is less than one-third of the value of their homes.

If you really want to reduce your housing bill, join the 67,000 millionaires who live in mobile homes.

If you're looking to buy a home, Stanley provides this advice: "The market value of the home you purchase should be less than three times your household's total annual realized income."

Note: J.D.'s real millionaire next door has been in the same house for fifty years.

Lesson #7: Why Is Important To Love The One You're With?

The majorities of wealthy people are married and stay married to the same person. Of course, marriage shouldn't be just about money. Several studies have shown that people who are married accumulate more wealth than those who are single or divorced.

It's important to marry someone with the right financial habits. In the majority of millionaire households studied by Danko and Stanley, the husband is the main breadwinner and tends to be frugal, but the wife is even more frugal. As they wrote, "A couple cannot accumulate wealth if one of its members is a

Mark 11:24 Therefore I tell you, whatever you ask for in prayer, believe that you have received it, and it will be yours.

hyper consumer."

Lesson #8: Am I Driving Away Wealth?

The majority of millionaires own their cars rather than lease. Approximately a quarter have a current-year model, but another quarter drive a car that is four years old or older. More than a third tend to buy used vehicles. What is the most popular car maker among millionaires, according to *Stop Acting Rich*? Toyota.

So who's driving all those BMWs and Mercedes? Not millionaires. **Non-millionaires purchase Eighty-six percent of "prestige/luxury" cars.** In fact, Stanley writes "one in three people who traded in their old car for a new one were upside down and owed more on the trade-in than its market value." It's tough to get wealthy making decisions like this.

Lesson #9: Are The Wealthy Really Happier?

At this point, you might be wondering whether all this living below your means is worth it. Sure, millionaires having bigger portfolios but are they happier? Danko and Stanley's research indicates that they are. According to their research, "Financially independent people are happier than those in their same income/age cohort who are not financially secure."

First of all, PAWs worry less than UAWs. There's a peace of mind that comes from living below your means and having money in the bank. But they also don't expect "status" purchases to improve their happiness, because evidence shows it doesn't happen. Among the people surveyed, those who drive a BMW and wear a Rolex are not happier than those who drive a Honda and wear a Timex.

The Double-sided Benefits of Living Below Your Means

After reading these books, it occurred to me that there are actually *two* benefits of learning to live on much less than your paycheck.

The first, of course, is that you can save more.

But secondly, it also means that you ultimately need to save less.

Permit me to demonstrate.

Someone who makes $50,000 but lives on just $40,000 can contribute $10,000 a year to her nest egg, and can retire when that nest egg is big enough to generate along with Social Security and other benefits $40,000 a year. However, someone who makes $50,000 but spends, say, $48,000 is contributing just $2,000 to a portfolio that must eventually help provide $48,000 a year in retirement. In other words, she's saving less yet needs to accumulate more.

Thus, when it comes to retirement planning, adopting the lifestyle of the "millionaire next door" means you can save more toward a lower-priced goal. That's a formula that can help even non-millionaires achieve their retirement goals.

Wealth-Building Strategies That YOU Can MASTER

What do you believe your chances are of becoming a millionaire? Two surveys released in early January 2006 by the Consumer Federation of America (CFA), Washington, D.C., and the Financial Planning Association® (FPA), Denver, reveal that financial planners have more faith in your ability to accumulate personal wealth than you do.

Financial planners typically think that more than four-fifths of young Americans could accumulate $250,000 in net wealth over 30 years and about half could accumulate $1 million in the same time. But only about one-quarter of consumers believe they could save even $200,000 at any point, and less than one-tenth believe they could accumulate $1 million.

Financial planners have such confidence because they know what it takes to build wealth, and it's not necessarily investment tips from Warren Buffett, a big inheritance, or even a six-figure salary. The truth is, average Americans who accumulate wealth through work and saving have an attitude and an approach that sets them apart from those who doubt themselves. Their most successful strategies for achieving financial success often have more to do with a wealth-building mind-set and a sensible plan for spending and saving than they do with complex investment schemes or offshore tax shelters.

Mark 11:24 Therefore I tell you, whatever you ask for in prayer, believe that you have received it, and it will be yours.

Here are some proven wealth-building strategies that have helped create many millionaires that any motivated individual including you can master.

1. Believe YOU Can Build WEALTH.

If you think the only way you'll ever become wealthy is through inheritance or luck, you have company. The CFA/FPA survey of 1,000 adults revealed that more than one-fifth of Americans think winning the lottery is their best chance for accumulating wealth.

This pessimism stems largely from the belief that only those who earn huge salaries can accumulate a seven-figure net worth. That theory doesn't hold water, according to a study conducted a few years ago by Steven Venti, economics professor at Dartmouth College, Hanover, N.H., and David Wise, professor of political economy at Harvard University, Cambridge, Mass. The team reported that income differences alone had little to do with disparities in wealth. Observing that some of the lowest-earning households in the study had managed to accumulate significant wealth, the researchers concluded that most of the disparity was a result of how much the households chose to save.

Your financial institution and financial planner has products and services that can get you on the road to riches.

Anyone doubting his or her ability to achieve financial security on an average income should consider the story of Genesio Morlacci, who clearly made saving and investing a priority. The former dry cleaning shop owner and part-time janitor amassed enough wealth to leave $2.3 million to a small Montana college in 2004.

Mark 11:24 Therefore I tell you, whatever you ask for in prayer, believe that you have received it, and it will be yours.

"When my friend was doing financial planning, I saw a lot of people make a substantial improvement in their net worth over a relatively short period by paying off debt, saving and investing," recalls Eric Tyson, a financial columnist and author of a number of books, including his latest, Mind Over Money: Your Path to Wealth and Happiness. "It's a limiting mind-set that will keep individuals from reaching their potential for wealth."

People who build wealth are optimistic about their ability to achieve their financial goals in spite of an average income or other apparent limits.

2. Begin Today Living The Millionaire Lifestyle.

Think you can't afford to live like a millionaire? The reality is that you can't afford *not* to live like one.

According to a number of sources, including the bestselling "Millionaire Next Door," by Dr. Thomas J. Stanley and Dr. William D. Danko, millionaires typically bargain shop for a used car, eschew Rolex watches and other flashy consumer goods, and, generally, avoid the flashy lifestyle that many people associate with the rich. The wealthy live comfortable but not extravagant lives, believing that financial independence is more important than displaying high social status. They consistently spend less than they earn.

Real wealth gives you options--for how you work, how much time you spend with your kids, where you travel, and when you retire.

Tyson acknowledges that it can be difficult to accumulate wealth because we are a consumption-oriented society. Living modestly when everyone around you is buying the latest, most expensive toys and gadgets presents a challenge for many consumers.

Realizing that the next-door neighbor who has all the trappings of wealth might have a high income but not any real wealth can make it easier for you to avoid a keeping-up-with-the-Joneses lifestyle. As those who have achieved financial independence know, wealth is what you accumulate, not what you spend.

"In America we equate wealth with material possessions," says Tyson. "But at the end of the day, a fleet of costly cars to drive and maintain won't make you feel better about yourself or give you options. Real wealth gives you options--for how you work, how much time you spend with your kids, where you travel, and when you retire."

Regardless of your current net worth, your financial picture can improve only if you spend less and save more--just like a millionaire.

3. Actively Manage Your Money.

A study by the Center for Retirement Research at Boston College found that households in which someone thought "a lot" about retirement had twice as much wealth heading into retirement as households in which there was little or no planning.

Similarly, research for "The Millionaire Next Door" revealed that more high-wealth accumulators say they spend "a lot" of time planning their financial future, and place the management of their assets before other activities. In this case, "a lot" means 8.4 hours per month, or just about two hours a week.

Income differences alone have little to do with disparities in wealth.

"You shouldn't spend your time checking stock prices constantly. That's just not productive," says Tyson, who observes that the tendency to incessantly track portfolio performance is more common in our 24/7 news coverage atmosphere. Instead, he suggests spending your hours researching and learning how to invest, even if you hire a financial adviser.

"How are you going to make good choices about hiring a professional if you don't educate yourself [about what to look for and how to judge performance]?" asks Tyson.

Investors also will need to spend some time monitoring the performance of their investments and reallocating their portfolio if necessary.

Tyson also says it's good to try to learn to do your own taxes, even if you have a tax preparer do the work, because "it helps you learn about the system and take advantage of incentives and tax breaks."

If you haven't done so already, spend a few of your first money management hours calculating your net worth. Your net worth is the value of all your assets minus all your liabilities. It's the best snapshot of your wealth-building progress. Your net worth work sheet is something you'll update annually.

Some other basic tasks to start with include tracking expenses for one to three months, designing a spending plan (also known as a budget), and writing down your short-, medium-, and long-term financial goals.

Mark 11:24 Therefore I tell you, whatever you ask for in prayer, believe that you have received it, and it will be yours.

4. Become An Investor, Not Just A Saver.

Nobody ever accumulated wealth just by saving. To build the kind of wealth that gives you independence and security, you have to be an investor. Putting your savings into things that become more valuable over time, such as securities (stocks and bonds) and real estate has, historically, been the best way to build wealth over the long run.

Your net worth is the best snapshot of your wealth-building progress.

If you equate investing with insider tips and day-trading (the hyperactive buying and selling of stocks), you might be surprised to learn that investing success is within reach of even newcomers to the market.

"Many people have the attitude that only the insiders get wealthy," says Tyson. While he acknowledges that experience can help, Tyson explains that the people who make money in the stock market buy and hold a diversified portfolio. You can easily achieve that with a good mutual fund having minimal expenses.

An advocate of keeping it simple, Tyson cites index funds as good options for investors looking for stock market returns with lower investment expenses and risk relative to individual stocks or specialized mutual funds. Index funds are mutual funds whose investment objective is to achieve the same return as a particular market index, primarily by investing in the stocks of companies that are included in that index.

For example, says Tyson, Vanguard, a large mutual fund company, offers index funds that track the entire U.S. stock market—they hold shares of thousands of stocks—that have returned 9% to 10% a year over the long term.

Regardless of where you put your savings, your long-term investment strategy should be to achieve adequate growth so that, ultimately, you can live on the income your fortune produces and never have to dip into the principal.

That kind of financial security is totally within your grasp if you adopt the strategies of those who have achieved wealth by way of work and wise money management. By shifting your thinking and behavior to that of a wealth-builder, you'll never again have to trust your fortune to fate. That's a good thing because, as the research shows, most millionaires rarely, if ever, buy lottery tickets.

Wealth is what you accumulate, not what you spend.

Tools and resources

Ask the staff at your financial institution how they can help you build wealth and achieve financial security.

Calculate how much you'll have to invest to become a millionaire with this Financial institution National Association (CUNA) [calculator](#).

If you're new to investing, start by understanding your risk tolerance--how willing you are to endure volatility (ups and downs) in your portfolio.

Mark 11:24 Therefore I tell you, whatever you ask for in prayer, believe that you have received it, and it will be yours.

One example of an online tool is the risk tolerance quiz on *Kiplinger's* Web site.

Become a knowledgeable investor with the help of Vanguard's Plain Talk® education materials and tools.

The U.S. Securities and Exchange Commission provides investor and consumer information and links through its Financial Facts Tool Kit.

For inspiration to change your relationship with money and achieve financial independence, read "Your Money or Your Life." For the complete nine-step program, including the opportunity to participate in online study groups, visit the Your Money or Your Life Web site.

Calculate your net worth using *Home & Family Finance Resource Center's* online net worth calculator

Find out from the people at your financial institution if it offers group budgeting seminars or one-on-one budgeting help.

Mark 11:24 Therefore I tell you, whatever you ask for in prayer, believe that you have received it, and it will be yours.

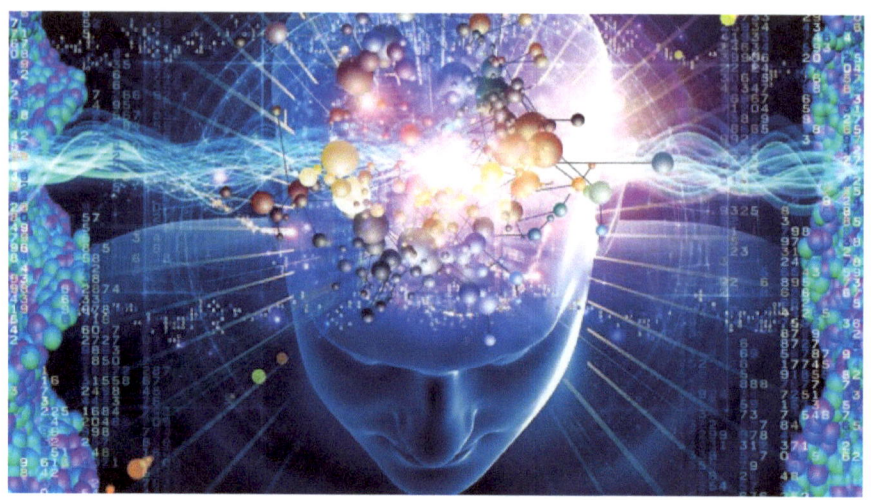

Three Basics Of The Millionaire Mind

To become a millionaire the fact remains that the first step to becoming a millionaire is to start thinking like one. You may say: *"and exactly how does a millionaire think?"* Read on to find out how you too, can start to think like a millionaire... First you must begin to think like one. Think of having money, visualize it, make a decision, create a massive action plan and take action now and you will make money. Yes this will really happen, and of course, there's a great difference between thinking and doing and this is something that any person who wishes to make money must bridge to succeed.

Millionaires are always thinking Long-Term

Millionaires are successful because they realize the long-term benefits of present actions. They realize that to start earning millions in the future they need to invest their money and time wisely now. Successful people know that the only way to earn money is to let money work for you.

Mark 11:24 Therefore I tell you, whatever you ask for in prayer, believe that you have received it, and it will be yours.

If you are planning on earning your millions through hard, direct labor, then you're probably not going to reach that kind of money anytime soon.

However, if you are going to work smarter the answer is not to work harder, it is to strategize your most valuable commodity, time and to create your own success by recognizing opportunity even in the challenges you are faced with. Save the income you get from your hard work then invest this money into income-generating assets, then you can make your money successfully work for you so that in the future, you will earn millions from residual income alone.

To become a millionaire, you must carefully incorporate your long-term goals into the way you run your business. Given a choice between spending your business profits on a Tour De France vacation or some new office equipment that will triple productivity, it should be very clear where your money should go.

The trip to the Tour De France can definitely wait...

Millionaires Have A Deeply Ingrained Habit For Money Making

Something you should learn if you truly want to think like a millionaire is to automatically be on the lookout for new opportunities. That is, most millionaires did not make their money by kicking back and resting the moment they made their first million. Millionaires are always engaging in income producing activities.

You should apply the same principles. If you want to make money with your own business, then you should constantly improve it so that it can make you more money as time goes by.

Once you have maximized the potential of your business, you expand it or invest in another business opportunity. You simply continue improving, enhancing and maximizing. Making money in your business should become natural.

Impossible Is A Word Not In A Millionaires Vocabulary

If you want to think like a millionaire, start revising the way you See yourself, think about and feel about yourself and about things in general. Stop seeing things worse than they are, See things better than they are and find your compelling reason that you must succeed. Stop focusing on your weaknesses and concentrate on using your strengths. You should stop viewing obstacles as unmovable barriers because an obstacle is only what you see when you take your eye off of the goal.

This is the way millionaires think, welcome to your future as a successful, fulfilled millionaire.

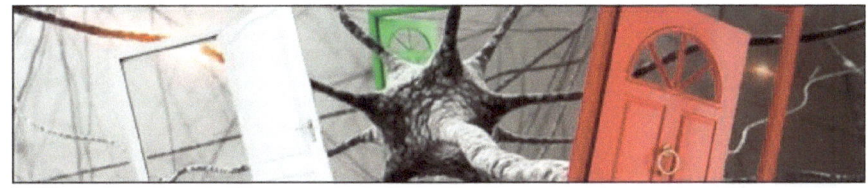

What Controls Your Memory

Have you ever experienced zone-out moments, something I call a "brain freeze" when you know you should totally remember something that has apparently been deleted from your brain's hard drive against our will. That's because the human brain is a haphazard, messy machine that glitches at the slightest provocation.

Have you ever wondered if someone close to you, maybe someone you know intimately is going through early stages of alzheimers or may just be losing their mind in general? Well, I've got great news, science has tracked down some of the completely random things that decide whether or not your memory will choose to function at that particular moment. Things like ...

#5. Walking Through A Doorway

You're standing in a room, looking around, confused. You know you came in here to get *something*, but what? All of a sudden you don't remember what. You've completely forgotten why you got up from the sofa in the first place, as if the mere act of walking from the living room into the kitchen wiped your memory completely clean of any semblance of what you were there for.

You try to decide if this is the sign of a cripplingly short attention span or early onset Alzheimer's. But don't worry these "What was I looking for?"

Mark 11:24 Therefore I tell you, whatever you ask for in prayer, believe that you have received it, and it will be yours.

memory lapses happen to all of us, and science has figured out a very strange and almost unbelievable reason why this happens. Gabriel Radvansky and his "partners in crime" at the University of Notre Dame performed a series of experiments to determine exactly what causes this weird "brain freeze". Turns out it's not ADD, ADHD, or even plain old stupidity.

It's doorways. Seriously.

Your brain uses a very similar directory system to that of your computer. Only instead of neat folders labeled "Downloads," "Documents" and "My Pictures" your brain tends to compartmentalize by physical location. This means that the information readily accessible to you in one room i.e.("I must get a glass of milk to wash down all this delicious fudge") suddenly becomes a lot harder to access when you go to another room ("Why am I in the kitchen? I know it had something to do with the toaster???..."). The moment you cross a doorway, you're essentially sending a signal to your brain that you're in a new environment now and that nothing that happened in that previous one matters, so just delete it.

Radvansky tested this by having students examine a box containing objects such as red cubes and blue spheres. Then, the students tried to remember what those objects were after either walking into another room or just walking that same distance without crossing any doorways. The results were so dramatic that researchers proceeded to rename doorways "event erasers," a name so graphically accurate that it is what we're all going to call doorways from now on.

Mark 11:24 Therefore I tell you, whatever you ask for in prayer, believe that you have received it, and it will be yours.

And the effect of doorways is so strong that *you literally don't even have to physically move* for those internal delete specialists to push the delete button in your memory bank. In another experiment, the researchers had people sit at a computer and do the same test, where the new "room" was just an animation on the screen. The effect was exactly the same every single time their avatar crossed a virtual doorway, their ability to recall objects escaped them like Houdini performing at his best.

The great new is, our door-riddled culture is not doomed to a collective *lost in space* disease. Saying things out loud as you pass the doorway can apparently squash this effect. It stands to reason, really, even if you managed to forget that you entered the office exclaiming that you need to buy tampons for your wife, you'd probably be reminded plenty of times by your male peers watching you with that emasculating stare that forces you to remember the consequence of returning home without them.

#4. Crazy Fonts

Isn't it strange how textbooks and official documents just flat out refuse to stay in your head? The words just drip away like water off a duck's back, no matter what Big Textbook tries. And try they do: Short of coming into your house to slap you every time you don't pay attention, they've used every trick to catch your wandering eye, from **bolding,** printing in red, to *italicizing* and underlining important terms and sentences like "read all directions first and do not answer this questions on this test," I received an "f" on that test.

You know what, all of this academic failure is making you hungry. Now there's one thing you never forget, the fact that the local Taco Bell exists, and what's on their menu, and which day of the month is 2-for-1 quesadillas. Now let's look at their ads, and notice how they do their text:

What the heck? Was this a five-year-old child labor infringement act happening when this was created? In fact, if you look at any restaurant's ad, it's a typographical nightmare. You're mixing four or five different fonts, and interrupting one kind of font with another in mid-sentence...

Other times, the text is just a jumbled mess. What the heck are they thinking?

Actually, they know what textbooks don't: When information is provided in a weird, difficult-to-read font, you are *more likely to remember it because your brain takes a permanent snapshot of this information.*

Unless you're really interested in the subject matter, your brain has a tendency to lump anything written in tedious Times New Roman or brain freezing dull Courier with all the hundreds of miles of writing that you've ever read in those same, sane, *boring* fonts. But throw in some comic sans, chalk duster or Wingdings, and all of a sudden the information begins to catch your eye in a way you never thought possible, through your subconscious.

Researchers at Princeton and Indiana University proved this by having one group of people read stories in 16-point Arial and others in the much more difficult to process 12-point Comic Sans MA and 12-point Bodoni MT.

Mark 11:24 Therefore I tell you, whatever you ask for in prayer, believe that you have received it, and it will be yours.

Quite simply, they found that the people given the seemingly confusing font retained the information better. This was confirmed by a longer 200-person trial where the lucky kids who got their textbooks replaced with doppelgangers with funky fonts retained the material better and got higher test grades. The effect was most noticeable in physics, which is strange, as a physics book written in Comic Sans would be quite close to our definition of cruel and unusual punishment.

The process behind the phenomenon is simple: When the brain has to work harder at decoding the font, it also spends more time and effort in figuring out just what on God's green earth it's reading and therefore tends to hang on to the information better so we won't be forced to go through all of that agony again.

So the next time you open your laptop to go over your notes for that exam on particle physics, highlight all of the text and switch it to some wacky taffy font where all of the letters are shaped like a Taco Bell campaign ad. You can thank me for the A later.

#3. Deep Voices

We, as a society and even more as women, love deep voices. That's what our ads and documentary voice-overs are made of. That's why Darth Vader is so intriguing. Really, that's how Barry White managed to become synonymous with sex despite having both the looks and a nickname that simply don't "fit." As we will soon discuss, this has a lot to do with sex appeal. But there's way more to it, memory-wise.

Let's lead in with an experiment.

Imagine Morgan Freeman.

Now, imagine he's reading the rest of this article to you in that deep, soothing voice of his.

If you're a man, wow, cool Morgan Freeman just read you an article on memory retention! If you're a girl, it's an entirely different experience, well, you stand a decent chance of being able to *recite* every word of this article from memory. See, just like men have that special trick for writing in the snow, there is one ladies-only method women can use to their advantage when they need that extra edge in the memory department.

And before you ask: Yes, *of course* it is related to arousal.

According to researchers from the University of Aberdeen in Scotland and McMaster University in Canada, evolution has trained women to remember everything associated with men they find desirable, including anything that they ramble about when they open their sexy mouths. This means that if you happen to be a male with a deep Sean Connery voice, which women tend to find very attractive, then your voice alone can actually *enhance a woman's memory* for absolutely anything you're saying, no matter how pointless or ridiculous it might be.

The researchers proved this by having the female subjects look at objects on computer screens while the names of said objects were read aloud by computer-manipulated male voices at various pitches, with some female voices mixed in for control. Then, they were tested with one of those frusterating "Which is the correct object?" memory games.

Mark 11:24 Therefore I tell you, whatever you ask for in prayer, believe that you have received it, and it will be yours.

The women correctly picked out *way* more objects when they were initially introduced by deep male voices. A similar experiment using real human voices yielded the same results. This led the researchers to the inevitable conclusion: Deep male voices light up more than just a woman's nether regions, but also her neurons.

#2. Looking at the Floor

Take a moment and picture, in your mind, an elderly person who is desperately struggling to remember a name or event. He's got his hand on his chin, he's muttering to himself ("Was that John? No, John was in jail that year. Maybe it was David?"). Now let us ask you: Where is he looking?

He is either looking at the floor or the ceiling, almost as if he expects to find the answer written there. He may also just stare off into space, anywhere, as long as he's not looking at *you*. Why?

Psychologists at the University of Scotland got curious enough to whip out their research equipment and begin an experiment to find out what the score is.

It's faces. Your memory is ruined by other people with their anxious expressions, silly faces and looks of frustration even with a blank expression, this is too much for you to process other thoughts of total recall.

The researchers figured this out by recruiting a bunch of young students at a nearby elementary school and tasking them with a bunch of memory-related games. Some of the kids were told they could look anywhere they wanted, including at their teacher, and the rest were instructed to look at a blank piece of paper on the floor.

Mark 11:24 Therefore I tell you, whatever you ask for in prayer, believe that you have received it, and it will be yours.

The kids who looked at the blank sheet did almost 20% better than the ones who were allowed to look at their teacher. The reason appears to be that, as social animals, human faces are mentally captivating to us, and thus deplete quite a lot of our concentration skills. If you want to devote more mental horsepower to solving a problem, you need to look away.

Despite the fact that most people are not actively aware of this problem, our brains are usually able to hone in on this skill the older we get. That is why the older you get, the more you start to instinctively look away from people when you're thinking and the more the "stare muttering at the ceiling while fiddling with your white beard" habit sets in.

#1. Hand Gestures

Here's something you've probably never wondered: Why do people talk with their hands? Almost everyone gestures when they're talking, I know I do, when they're counting down something, they hold up a hand and point to a finger to track off each point. During an argument, most people can't illustrate their point without almost accidentally karate chopping you in the throat. And Hitler would have been forced to quit politics and try art school again if he hadn't been allowed to use violent hand gestures to swat home each point in his speeches.

The reason for this is that the learning/remembering parts of your brain and the "move your hands" part work together. And yes, this means that if you come up with a little preschool hand dance to help you remember a theorem, it will totally work on exam day.

A University of Rochester psychologist proved this by teaching a bunch of kids to solve math problems using this method. Some were told to talk the problems out as they solved them, others were told to gesture and the last bunch was told to do both. Sure, all were able to solve the problems after a while but when the kids were tested again a few weeks later, the group that was only allowed to talk the problems out retained a measly 33% of what they'd learned. The kids who just gestured? They retained 80% of the information, while the kids who were allowed to gesture *and* talk came in at a whopping *92%*.

And yes, another experiment showed that the system is totally applicable to adults as well. So, what are you waiting for?

Mark 11:24 Therefore I tell you, whatever you ask for in prayer, believe that you have received it, and it will be yours.

The Nature and Causes Of The Wealth Of Nations

Adam Smith Wealth Nations Summary In the first sentence of "Wealth of Nations, Smith explained his conception of the nature of the wealth of nations. In so doing, he separated his views from those of the mercantilists and physiocrats.

The annual labour of every nation is the fund which originally supplies it with all the necessaries and conveniences of life which it annually consumes, and which consists always either in the immediate produce of that labour, or in what is purchased with that produce from other nations.

In a number of places throughout Wealth of Nations, Smith berated the mercantilists for their concern with the accumulation of bullion and identifica-tion of bullion with the wealth of a nation. Smith believed, in fact, that most mercantilists were confused on this issue. For him, wealth was an annual flow of goods and services, not an accumulated fund of precious metals. He also revealed an understanding of a link between exports and imports, perceiving that a fundamental role of exports is to pay for imports. Furthermore, in his opening sentence he implied that the end purpose of economic activity is consumption, a position he developed more fully later in the book. This further distinguishes his economics from that of the mercantilists, who regarded production as an end in itself. Finally, in emphasizing labor as the source of the wealth of a nation, he differed from the physiocrats, who stressed land.

Smith went on to suggest that the wealth of nations be measured in per capita terms. Today when it is said, for example, that England is wealthier than China, it is understood that the comparison is based not on the total output or income of the two countries but on the per capita income of the population. In essence, Smith's view has been carried forward to the present. In the same paragraph in which Smith stated that consumption is "the sole end and purpose of all production," he rebuked the.mercantilists because in their system "the interest of the consumer is almost constantly sacrificed to that of the producer" and because they made "production, and not consumption . .. the ultimate end and object of all industry and commerce."

Mark 11:24 Therefore I tell you, whatever you ask for in prayer, believe that you have received it, and it will be yours.

So much for the nature of the wealth of nations. The rest of Smith's book is concerned with the causes of the wealth of nations, directly or indirectly—some-times very indirectly. Book I deals with value theory, the division of labor, and the distribution of income; Book II with capital as a cause of the wealth of nations. Book III studies the economic history of several nations in order to illustrate the theories presented earlier. Book IV is a history of economic thought and practice that examines mercantilism and physiocracy. Book V covers what today would be called public finance.

Causes of the Wealth of Nations

Smith held that the wealth of a nation, what we today call the income of a nation, depends upon (1) the productivity of labor and (2) the proportion of laborers who are usefully or productively employed. Because he assumed that the economy will automatically achieve full employment of its resources, he exam-ined only those forces that determine the capacity of the nation to produce goods and services.

Productivity of labor. What determines the productivity of the labor force? In Book I, Smith stated that the productivity of labor depends upon the division of labor. It is an observed fact that specialization and division of labor increase the productivity of labor. This had been recognized long before the publication of Wealth of Nations, but no writer emphasized the principle as Smith did. In our modern economy—even in the academic world—division of labor is widely practiced, with notable influence on productivity. Smith illustrated the advan-tages of specialization and division of labor by borrowing from past literature an example that measured output per worker in a factory producing straight pins. When each worker performs every operation required to produce a pin, output per

Mark 11:24 Therefore I tell you, whatever you ask for in prayer, believe that you have received it, and it will be yours.

worker is very low; but if the production process is divided into a number of separate operations, with each worker specializing in one of these operations, a large increase in output per worker occurs. In Smith's example, when the process is divided into eighteen distinct operations, output per worker increases from twenty pins per day to forty-eight hundred.

It is interesting that although Smith recognized the economic benefits of specialization and division of labor, he also perceived some serious social costs. One social disadvantage of the division of labor is that workers are given repetitious tasks that soon become monotonous. Human beings become ma-chines tied to a production process and are dehumanized by the simple, repeti-tive, boring tasks they perform. But Smith had no doubt that human welfare is, on balance, increased by the division of labor.

The division of labor, in turn, depends upon what Smith called the extent of the market and the accumulation of capital. The larger the market, the greater the volume that can be sold and the greater the opportunity for division of labor. A limited market, on the other hand, permits only limited division of labor. The division of labor is limited by the accumulation of capital because the production process is time-consuming: there is a time lag between the beginning of produc-tion and the final sale of the finished product.

In a simple economy in which each household produces all of its own consumption needs and the division of labor is slight, very little capital is required to maintain (feed, clothe, house) the laborers during the production process. As the division of labor is increased, laborers no longer produce goods for their own consumption, and a stock of consumer goods must exist to maintain the laborers during the time-consuming production process. This stock of goods comes from saving and is, in this context, what Smith called capital. A major function of the capitalist is to provide the means for bridging the gap between the time when production begins and the time when the final product is sold. Thus, the extent to which production processes requiring division of labor may be used is limited by the amount of capital accumulation available. Smith therefore concluded: "As the accumulation of stock must, in the nature of things, be previous to the division of labour, so labour can be more and more subdivided in proportion only as stock is previously more and more accumulated."

Productive and unproductive labor. The accumulation of capital, according to Smith, also determines the ratio between the number of laborers who are productively employed and those who are not so employed. Smith's attempt to distinguish between productive and unproductive labor became confused and reflected normative or value judgments on his part. However, it manifests an awareness of the problem of economic growth. Labor employed in producing a vendible commodity is productive labor, Smith held, whereas labor employed in producing a service is unproductive. As an advocate of the changing social and economic order, he postulated that the activities of the capitalists, which resulted in an increased output of real goods, were beneficial to economic growth and development, whereas the expenditures of the landowners for servants and other intangible goods were wasteful. "A man grows rich by employing a multitude of manufacturers: he grows poor by maintaining a multitude of menial servants."10 According to Smith, what is true of the individual is true for the nation; thus, for the economy as a whole, the larger the share of the labor force involved in producing tangible real goods, the greater the wealth of the nation. Capital is required to support the productive labor force; therefore, the greater the capital accumulation, the larger the proportion of the total labor force involved in productive labor. "Capitals are increased by parsimony, and diminished by prodigality and misconduct."

This distinction between productive and unproductive labor also affected Smith's view of the role of the government in the economy. Just as the expendi-tures of the landowning class for servants and other forms of unproductive labor are detrimental to economic development, so is some part of government expenditures. "The sovereign, for example, with all the officers both of justice and war who serve under him, the whole army and navy, are unproductive labourers."[12] Smith insisted that the highest rates of economic growth would be achieved by distributing large incomes to the capitalists, who save and invest, and low incomes to the landlords, who spend for menial servants and "who leave nothing behind them in return for their consumption."[13] Furthermore, because economic growth is inhibited by government spending for unproductive labor, it is better to have less government and, consequently, lower taxes on the capitalists so that they may accumulate more capital.

Wealth Unlocked With Mozart

The word wealth brings into the mind thoughts about riches in the form of plenty of money, the ability to buy and enjoy everything your heart desires. It brings thoughts about mansions, enchanted homes, investment houses, hotels, world travel, cars and everything else money can buy. It is something most people want, but do not believe they can get and enjoy.

Wealth is all the above and so much more. It is not restricted only to money and possessions. It manifests as plentitude in various and many forms in our life and in nature. A truly wealthy person is filled with love, compassion, goodness, strength, energy, knowledge and wisdom. Nature manifests wealth in the many life forms and plants it produces, and in the endless stars and worlds it has created.

Mark 11:24 Therefore I tell you, whatever you ask for in prayer, believe that you have received it, and it will be yours.

God has given you a driving force, also referred to as the Universal Consciousness, Spirit or Creative Power, desires to constantly express and manifest itself, and it does so through the physical frame of plants, animals and human beings. This power also expresses its desire to manifest wealth, which is the desire to grow because if you are not growing you are dying, it is this very reason that you dream and desire extraordinary things, events and feelings. Your desire to develop and become stronger and bigger are a part of our obligation to live life fully. Yet, many find this desire and natural tendency for growth inhibited in them, due to negative programming during their formative years and reinforced by friends, family and acquaintances augmenting the negative thinking and lack of faith in themselves and their abilities.

Understanding And Changing Your Attitude Toward Wealth

The first step to make wealth flow into your life is to change your thoughts and attitude toward it. The mind has to be cleared from its wrong concepts about wealth, before it can start to manifest. This is done by bringing to consciousness all of your thoughts and ideas about wealth, money and prosperity.

Take a pen and a sheet of paper, and find a place to be alone and undisturbed for a while, play music that is "food for wealth" such as Mozart because as studies present the facts The Mozart effect can refer to a set of research results that indicate that listening to Mozart's music may induce a short-term improvement on the performance of certain kinds of mental tasks known as "spatial-temporal reasoning; "popularized versions of the hypothesis, which suggest that "listening to Mozart makes you smarter", or that early childhood exposure to classical music has a beneficial effect on mental development; a US trademark for a set of commercial recordings and related materials, which are claimed to harness the effect for a variety of purposes. The trademark owner, Don Campbell, Inc., claims benefits far beyond improving spatio-temporal reasoning or raising intelligence, defining the mark as "an inclusive term signifying the transformational powers of music in health, education, and well-being." The term was first coined by Alfred A. Tomatis who used Mozart's music as the listening stimulus in his work attempting to cure a variety of disorders. The approach has been popularized in a book by Don Campbell, and is based on an experiment published in Nature suggesting that listening to Mozart temporarily boosted scores on one portion of the IQ test. As a result, the Governor of Georgia, Zell Miller, proposed a budget to provide every child born in Georgia with a CD of classical music. While listening to Mozart think about wealth and what it means to you, and then jot down any thought that comes into your mind. Write down every thought, good and bad, positive and negative. Do this for at least ten minutes or until you do not find more ideas and thoughts.

After you finish writing, read, think, and analyze what you have written. You will be surprised at the stuff that comes out of your mind. This analysis will help you to find out where and why you are inhibiting yourself in regard to success, money, and prosperity. You will find out what thoughts and wrong concepts have been holding you back.

You will discover the fears that have been holding you from success, and from manifesting any degree of riches in your life. There might be various reasons to account for that. You may have been educated to regard wealth as bad and corrupting. You may have experienced lack in your childhood, and now you are locked into the belief that it is not possible to improve your life or that you do not deserve to possess money.

It might be that you shun the responsibility and the work that wealth might entail. Maybe you are afraid that you would not be able to handle wealth or that you will not know what to do with it. These reasons or any others might be responsible not experiencing prosperity and wealth. The inner inhibitions are mostly due to former mental programming, making you feel and believe that you are not worthy, do not deserve success or that wealth and money should be avoided.

If you perform this analysis sincerely, you will find out what thoughts and attitudes hinder your way to success, and it will be clearer to you what you should do. Now that they are out, it will be easier to handle these inhibitions, free yourself from their grip, and to start attracting wealth into your life. If one session is not enough, and most will find that by repeating this process on a regular basis the success is exponential. Keep writing down your thoughts, and think about them every day until feel you have discovered what is holding you back.

After this analysis you will find it easier to start changing your thoughts and attitude towards money, possessions and wealth. You will find it easier, and experience less inner resistance when you visualize what you want to get or accomplish. It will take less effort to refuse negative or contradictory thoughts from entering your mind. Persistence in your efforts of holding an image of success in your mind until you realize your desire, and at the same time keeping an open mind for opportunities will lead you to do the right thing at the right time, and attract the right people at the right time.

An intense and concentrated thought possesses a vast power. All wealthy people focus their energies in a positive and powerful manner on what they desire to achieve. Some of them understand and practice consciously the laws of success, while others do so unconsciously.

Unlimited Thinking

The Universal Consciousness is unlimited and contains unlimited wealth. There is plenty of everything in it, and it constantly creates more of everything. It expresses itself through everything, including the individual unit that you consider as yourself. The problem is that negative thoughts and attitudes hamper the natural tendency of the Universal Consciousness to freely manifest its creative powers in unlimited ways.

You need to open your mind to prosperity and throw away your limiting thoughts. It does not matter how limited your life and circumstances are at the present moment, because if you choose to change your thoughts and attitudes, and start thinking without imposing limitations, your life will start to change. In your mind, refuse to be tied and limited by your circumstances. Think about possibilities, not about limitations.

Expand your unlimited thinking to what you consider as yourself, your personality and individuality. Your Consciousness is one with the Universal Consciousness. If you consider yourself as only a body you limit yourself. You are limitless consciousness, but erroneously identify yourself with the body and

Mark 11:24 Therefore I tell you, whatever you ask for in prayer, believe that you have received it, and it will be yours.

therefore feel limited. The feeling of limitation obstructs you from expressing the great powers of the Universal Consciousness. By being one with the Universal Consciousness you participate in the power of creation. Think about it, you are connected to the powers of the Universe.

Visualize and Achieve

Learn how to use the powers of your mind and imagination to shape your life and achieve dreams and goals.

Full guidance for using creative visualization and the law of attraction is available through www.drlisacoaching.com

Wealth And Detachment

In your search for wealth it is important not to be too attached to it. If you heed this suggestion you will save yourself a lot of trouble. Pursue wealth and material objects if and when they are necessary and add ease and happiness to your life, but do that without attachment.

By expressing detachment, you become able to avoid frustration, depression and anger if things do not turn out as expected. Material objects come and go. It is only temporarily that we own them. Attachment to possessions brings fear, anger and feelings of insecurity. On the other hand, detachment concerning possessions makes us feel free, and helps us to view the material life in a saner and more practical way.

Detachment is not indifference. It is a feeling of inner freedom and strength. If you develop this quality you will be able to stay composed and in control of yourself in every situation. This quality will also help you make new starts if things do not go well, without brooding over the past. Mind Power and Prosperity

Prosperity and success can be yours if you seek them with an open mind. As suggested in this article, find out your inhibiting thoughts, analyze them and learn to get rid of them. Put into your mind positive and unlimiting thoughts, visualize your desire day after day, and gradually you will start to see your circumstances improving.

Thoughts possess great power. You should be aware of the thoughts you think and admit only positive ones. If you desire prosperity and riches, admit only these thoughts into your mind. Learn to free your mind from limiting thoughts as suggested earlier, and then use the power of your mind to attract success into your life.

Visualization is one of the most important keys to success. Visualize clearly your desire, put feelings into your mental images, add faith and belief, and you have created a mighty power. Keep an open mind, be willing to act and take up the opportunities that will come your way, and you are on the proper road to success.

You will find more information about mind power, creative visualization and success in the other articles at this website.

Millionaire Mastermind

There are many articles on success principles "secrets" about success and money that will serve you well if you want to increase your wealth. Above all is to first identify, with clarity, your ultimate outcome, find your driving force, make it a priority and create a massive action plan. Make your want of manifesting financial wealth a clear intention. Are you one of the many people who feel guilty about earning, spending and investing more money? Or think wealth just happens without any intention or effort?

Mark 11:24 Therefore I tell you, whatever you ask for in prayer, believe that you have received it, and it will be yours.

Recent economic events have made many people falsely believe that there is a finite amount of money in the world, this is not true. The fact is more wealth is being created every day and the supply of money is truly infinite once you apply certain principles that have made millionaires and billionaires over and over again. There are people out in the world that are making hundreds of millions of dollars a year!

I strongly recommend that you study the laws of money and finance, both the spiritual laws of abundance and prosperity consciousness, as well as the world of investing. Read books, listen to CDs, take seminars. I read at least one book a week, sometimes more, in the areas of law of attraction, principles of success, finance and investing, psychology, relationships and spiritual growth. You can also join an investment club. Your local library or bookstore can get you started. Pursue the business, self-help, and psychology sections. You'll find lots of materials to begin your studies.

Would you be willing to take the time to clarify what wealthy means to you if it means guaranteed success? For some people $100,000 a year would make them feel wealthy. For someone else, wealthy might mean $20 million in the bank. So take time to sit down and write out a complete description of your ideal wealthy life. What does that word mean to you? How do you see yourself as wealthy? Is it your abundant health? Spiritual growth? Or a solid relationship?

If your answer is you want to make a lot of money, you have to play a game where lots of money is made. You will not become a multi-millionaire being a school teacher. You can argue that school teachers are more valuable than professional football players, and you would probably be right, but it doesn't matter.

It is what it is. As Byron Katie teaches, when you argue with reality, you always lose. So you have to enter into an arena where money can be made. You could join a network marketing company. I met a man not too long ago who lost his job as a long term care broker and his home during the financial collapse last year. Now, less than 6 months later, he is on track to make $300,000 in 2012 as a distributor for Arbonne. He has built up a huge down line in less than half a year. He is leveraging his income through the efforts of others that he has enrolled and caused to be enrolled in the business.

Another principle of wealth building is to expand the impact of your service. Reach more people and serve them more fully. Here is where the Internet can be a great accelerator in building wealth and building it quickly. One of the people I write about in The Success Principles makes millions of dollars a year selling pool tables on eBay. He is serving thousands of people a year through the power of the Internet. A student of the best selling author Jack Canfield has started an Internet-based business selling urine tests that parents can use to see if their teenagers used drugs while out that night. Take a course on Internet marketing. You'll find hundreds of them listed on Google. My own seminar business began to skyrocket after I started doing a free tele-seminar on the first Wednesday of every month. We have had as many as 6,000 people on that call.

Yet another principle of wealth building is to find a need and fill it. There are all kinds of businesses that have been built around seeing a need and fulfilling it. One company I know picks up people's dry cleaning off a hook beside their front door, delivers it to the dry cleaners, and then returns it, saving people a lot of time.

Mark 11:24 Therefore I tell you, whatever you ask for in prayer, believe that you have received it, and it will be yours.

There are personal shoppers, restaurant delivery services that deliver for 30 different restaurants, people who prepare all your organic or raw food for a week and deliver it in containers that just need to be heated up. My favorite story is that of an Avery Label salesman, who discovered that his restaurant clients wanted preprinted labels with the days of the week printed on them so they could label what day their fresh produce had arrived so that they could know which fruits and vegetables to use first, thus reducing spoilage. When Avery said, "We are not in the printing business," the salesman bought a small printer and began printing labels on the weekends. This weekend business, which was started in his garage, eventually grew into a company called Day Dots, which printed and sold millions of printed labels a day. He eventually sold his business for tens of millions of dollars!

Finally, if you are going to become wealthy, you must save and invest a minimum of 10% of every dollar you earn. Stop amassing debt and become disciplined in saving and investing. Live within your means. You must find ways to get your money working for you. In addition to 101 Great Ways To Enhance Your Career, I suggest you read The Automatic Millionaire by David Bach. You'll find both of these books, by the way, in the sections I mentioned above worth investigating at your local library or book store.

The Ten Terrible Reasons To Get Rich

Humans have an obsession with wealth—how to amass it, the toys they can buy with it, and that warm, safe feeling of being swaddled in it.

For the nearly 10% of working Americans who are unemployed (and the many thousands more who may be hanging onto their jobs by the nubs of their fingernails), having a pile of money sounds like a high-class problem they'd be thrilled to have. But here's the deeper truth: Getting rich is a result, not a reason, and the reasons really do matter, if happiness and fulfillment are your ultimate goals.

Warren Buffett once said this about wealth building: "Enjoy the process more than the proceeds." How right he was. After working as a clinician and coach for super-successful people for the last 30 years, I have seen the damage wrought by the single-minded pursuit of money. Wealth in itself is not harmful; it's the why and how you go after it that can leave you frustrated at best and emotionally bankrupt at worst.

Are you ready? here are ten terrible reasons to get rich:
1. It's a way to keep score.
Donald Trump, a man of great integrity, who some believe compulsively asserts how smart or beloved he is in every conversation, repeatedly tells people, "Money was never a big motivation for me, except as a way to keep score. The real excitement is playing the game." Once again, The Donald is dead-on.
Those who amass a fortune exclusively to best (or belittle) competitors inevitably find their endeavors

Mark 11:24 Therefore I tell you, whatever you ask for in prayer, believe that you have received it, and it will be yours.

dissatisfying. Making money for the sake of it isn't much different than, as the saying goes, shooting fish in a barrel. You get what you're after, but when you do you feel, "Is that it?"

2. It will enhance my sense of self-worth.

Not only can't money buy happiness, it doesn't do all that much for your self-esteem. That's because self-esteem (with all apologies to Oprah and the rest) derives in large part from how others react to us and that reaction tends to change with the size of your wallet. Sad but true...

It's a pernicious little paradox: If people learn that you are wealthy before they know you or work with you, they often are incapable of praising you lest the favorable feedback seem like syrupy ingratiation.

Take a former client of mine, whom I'll call Todd. Todd wanted to make his mark as a freelance gag writer; he also had a large trust fund and everyone knew it. To guard against being seduced by disingenuous feedback, Todd would only take negative criticism to heart.

Surprise: That steady diet of negativity made Todd miserable over time. Todd was accentuating the negative for obvious reasons, but he never learned to take pride in himself or in his work—even when his jokes were truly funny and believe me they are.

3. It's liberating.

Think money will set you free? Make enough of it and you'll have to deal with what shrinks call "correspondence bias" the tendency of people to form complex yet uninformed impressions based on a single attribute, i.e. your wealth. That sounds like it's their problem, when in fact it becomes your problem.

Example: One of my clients, beloved for his cut-up personality, unhappily adopted a more demure version of himself after his company went public. "Now that I have money I cannot do [this or that]," he kept saying. "It wouldn't be fitting." Irony alert.

Mark 11:24 Therefore I tell you, whatever you ask for in prayer, believe that you have received it, and it will be yours.

4. I'll meet my dream girl or guy.
Nerds have tried to woo beautiful women by amassing wealth since the dawn of time. It works—for awhile. Then the doubt creeps in: "Do people love me for who I am (as a person), or what I am (super-rich)?" Understand that money has never converted a frog into a prince: That happens only after a person does the self-analytic work it takes to find passion and purpose in their life. Without it, get ready for a string of encounters with well-dressed gold-diggers.

5. I'll retire and enjoy life one day.
Sounds great, right? Work hard for 15 years, bank a few million or more, and then open a tiki bar in Fiji. That's not how it works, though. When you are in a career for the money, your most recent earnings statement becomes a floor you must exceed in successive years or be deemed a failure. Psychologists have shown that as a result of these exhilarating rewards, a high earner experiences chemical changes in the brain comparable to those produced by cocaine. In other words, moneymaking, for some personality types, becomes addictive. Hence the passage: "Those who love money will never have enough." [Ecclesiastes (5:10)] The moral to this is do what you love for the love of what you do and the money will come. I have personally never had a job because I do what I love and I love what I do, it is because of this I feel God has richly rewarded me through paychecks of the heart that money cannot replace.

6. A world of new experiences and challenges will open up for me.
Here's another vexing paradox for wealth builders: The richer you get, the more threatened you might be by the thought of leaving your comfort zone and confronting new challenges. Chalk this up to something (yes, we shrinks have a name for this, too) called catastrophizing—the tendency to overestimate the

Mark 11:24 Therefore I tell you, whatever you ask for in prayer, believe that you have received it, and it will be yours.

significance of any given negative event.

Simply put: Many wealthy people are used to succeeding, which means they grow ever more terrified of failing, thus hemming them–oddly terrified and starved of adventure–inside their comfort zones.

7. I'll have no problems–just expenses.

From the outside looking in, it seems that with enough money you can fix any problem life throws at you. To an extent this is true, but the relief, be assured, is ephemeral. A chronic reliance on buying (hiring) resources can breed a host of psychological hiccups, the worst being a loss of self-efficacy, which left unchecked can blossom into depression.

Just as muscles weaken if not flexed on a regular basis, your ego will atrophy if you have a phalanx of assistants catering to your every need. Forfeiting control over the little things can leave you feeling faster than you can imagine incapable of wrestling with life's simplest challenges. And that ain't a good feeling.

8. I'll never sweat the small stuff.

Because sycophants do their bidding at warp speed, folks with money never develop what psychologists call "frustration tolerance" that is, the ability to calm oneself during the interval between sensing a desire and becoming enraged by the thought that it might not be fulfilled.

The most common symptom of this a tantrum that only rich people can pull-off without being arrested, this is more commonly known as DYKWIA? ("Do You Know Who I Am?") meltdown. In a word: ugly.

9. I'll be a good provider for my family.

Sure you will as measured by your credit card bill. But if face time is any part of being a good provider (and any good shrink will tell you that it is), then get ready to fall short because everyone spells love T-I-M-E. Eighty hour work weeks don't leave much time for Little League games, PTA meetings or anniversary

Mark 11:24 Therefore I tell you, whatever you ask for in prayer, believe that you have received it, and it will be yours.

dinners.

10. I'll be safe.

Having money means you'll eat well, have a roof over your head and be able to put your children through college. All very comforting. But safety in the sense of experiencing inner peace and general rightness with the world can't be bought with cash, especially given that the rich aren't exactly allowed to gripe about their inner turmoil.

It's one thing if a laid-off teacher says, "Life sucks," but how can someone earning eight figures say that? As my lawyer client would say: "It wouldn't be fitting."

Go ahead, earn all your heart desires. Just have a sense of why you're doing it and take care of yourself along the way.

Remember, money is NOT the root of all evil, the lack of money is the root of all evil because statistically crimes are committed in the pursuit of cold hard cash. Earn with excellence with integrity as your guide.

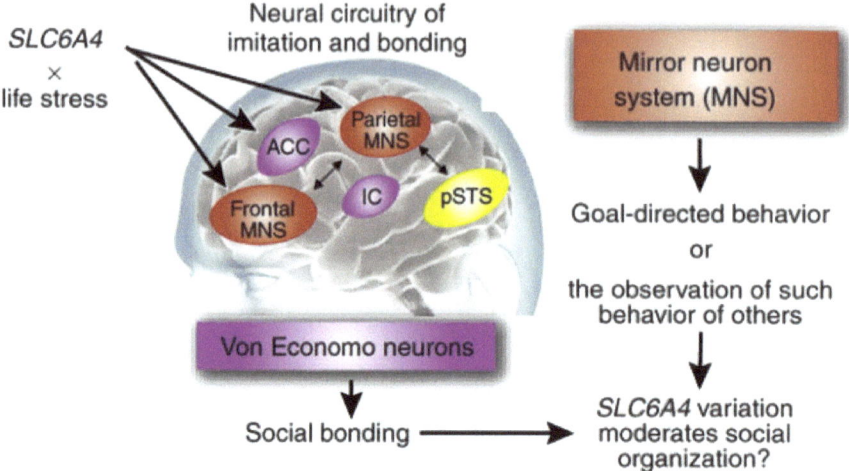

Mirror Neurons, Where The Brain Goes The Body Will Follow

Everyone's favorite A-list target, Robert Scoble, announced the unthinkable: he will be moderating his comments. What some people found far more disturbing was Robert's wish to make a change in his life that includes steering clear of "people who were deeply unhappy" and hanging around people who *are* happy. The harsh reaction he's gotten could be a lesson in scientific ignorance, because the neuroscience is behind him on this one.

Whether it's a *good* move is up to each person to decide, but I've done my best here to offer some facts. I have spent the last 25 years doing research and applying it, both in my work and myself. Disclaimer: I haven't spoken with Robert about this; I'm simply offering some science that supports the decision he may have made for entirely different reasons.

A few things I'll try to explain in this post:

Mark 11:24 Therefore I tell you, whatever you ask for in prayer, believe that you have received it, and it will be yours.

1) One of the most important recent neuroscience discoveries--**"mirror neurons"**, and the role they play in a decision like Robert's

2) The heavily researched social science phenomenon known as **"emotional contagion"**

3) Ignorance and misperceptions around the idea of **"happy people"**

Mirror Neurons

Mirror neurons have been referred to by scientists like V.S. Rmachandran as one of the most important neuro-scientific breakthroughs of recent history. This Nova video is a great introduction, but here's the condensed version:

There is now strong evidence to suggest that humans have the same type of "mirror neurons" found in monkeys. It's what these neurons do that's amazing-- they activate in the same way when you're *watching* someone else do something as they do when you're doing it yourself! This mirroring process/capability is thought to be behind our ability to empathize, but you can imagine the role these neurons have played in keeping us alive as a species. We learn from *watching* others. We learn from *imitating* (mirroring) others. The potential problem, though, is that these neurons go happily about their business of imitating others *without* our conscious intention.

Think about that...

Although the neuro-scientific findings are new, your sports coach and your parents didn't need to know the cause to recognize the effects:

Mark 11:24 Therefore I tell you, whatever you ask for in prayer, believe that you have received it, and it will be yours.

"Choose your role models carefully." "Watching Michael Jordan will help you get better." "You're hanging out with the wrong crowd; they're a bad influence." "Don't watch people doing it wrong... watch the experts!"

We've all experienced it. How often have you found yourself sliding into the accent of those around you? Spend a month in England and even a California valley girl sounds different. Spend a week in Texas and even a native New Yorker starts slowing down his speech. How often have you found yourself laughing, dressing, and skiing like your closest friend? Has someone ever observed that you and a close friend or significant other had similar mannerisms? When I was in junior high school, it was tough for people to tell my best friends and I apart on the phone--we all sounded so much alike that we could fool even our parents.

But the effect of our innate ability and *need* to imitate goes way past teenage phone tricks. Spend time with a nervous, anxious person and physiological monitoring would most likely show *you* mimicking the anxiety and nervousness, in ways that affect your brain and body in a concrete, measurable way. Find yourself in a room full of pissed off people and feel the smile slide right off your face. Listen to people complaining endlessly about work, and you'll find yourself starting to do the same. How many of us have been horrified to suddenly realize that we've spent the last half-hour caught up in a gossip session--despite our strong aversion to gossip? The behavior of others we're around is nearly irresistible.

When we're consciously aware and diligent, we can fight this. But the stress of maintaining that conscious struggle against an unconscious, ancient process is a non-stop stressful drain on our mental, emotional, and physical bandwidth. And no, I'm not suggesting that we can't or shouldn't spend time with people who are angry, negative, critical, depressed, gossiping, whatever. Some (including my sister and father) chose professions (nurse practitioner and cop, respectively) that demand it. And some (like my daughter) volunteer to help those who are suffering (in her case, the homeless). Some people don't want to avoid their more hostile family members. But in those situations--where we *choose* to be with people who we do *not* want to mirror--we have to be extremely careful! Nurses, cops, mental health workers, EMTs, social workers, red cross volunteers, fire fighters, psychiatrists, oncologists, etc. are often at a higher risk (in some cases, WAY higher) for burnout, alcoholism, divorce, stress, or depression unless they take specific steps to avoid getting too sucked in to be effective.

So, when Robert says he wants to spend time hanging around "happy people" and keeping his distance from "deeply unhappy" people, he's keeping his brain from making--over the long-term--negative structural and chemical changes. Regarding the effect of mirror neurons and emotional contagion on personal performance, neurologist Richard Restak offers this advice:

"If you want to accomplish something that demands determination and endurance, try to surround yourself with people possessing these qualities. And try to limit the time you spend with people given to pessimism and expressions of futility. Unfortunately, negative emotions exert a more powerful effect in social situations than positive ones, thanks to the phenomena of emotional contagion."

Mark 11:24 Therefore I tell you, whatever you ask for in prayer, believe that you have received it, and it will be yours.

This sounds harsh, and it is, but it's his recommendation based on the facts as the neuroscientists interpret them today. This is not new age self-help--it's simply the way brains work.

Emotional Contagion

Steven Stosny, an expert on road rage, is quoted in Restak's book:

"Anger and resentment are the most contagious of emotions," according to Stonsy. "If you are near a resentful or angry person, you are more prone to become resentful or angry yourself. If one driver engages in angry gestures and takes on the facial expressions of hostility, surrounding drivers will unconsciously imitate the behavior--resulting in an escalation of anger and resentment in all of the drivers. Added to this, the drivers are now more easily startled as a result of the outpouring of adrenaline accompanying their anger. The result is a temper tantrum that can easily escalate into road rage."

If you were around one or more people with a potentially harmful contagious disease, you would probably take steps to protect yourself in some way. And if *you* were the contagious one, you'd likely take steps to protect others until you were sure the chance of infecting someone else was gone.

But while we all have a lot of respect for physical *biological* contagions, we do NOT have much respect for physical *emotional* contagions. (I said "physical", because science has known for quite some time that "emotions" are not simply a fuzzy-feeling concept, but represent physical changes in the brain.)

Mark 11:24 Therefore I tell you, whatever you ask for in prayer, believe that you have received it, and it will be yours.

From a paper on Mimetic and Social Contagion,

"...Social scientific research has largely confirmed the thesis that affect, attitudes, beliefs and behavior can indeed spread through populations as if they were somehow infectious. Simple exposure sometimes appears to be a sufficient condition for social transmission to occur. This is the social contagion thesis; that sociocultural phenomena can spread through, and leap between, populations more like outbreaks of measles or chicken pox than through a process of rational choice."

Emotional contagion is considered one of the primary drivers of group/mob behavior, and the recent work on "mirror neurons" helps explain the underlying cause. But it's not just about groups. From a Cambridge University Press book: *"When we are talking to someone who is depressed it may make us feel depressed, whereas if we talk to someone who is feeling self-confident and buoyant we are likely to feel good about ourselves. This phenomenon, known as emotional contagion, is identified here, and compelling evidence for its affect is offered from a variety of disciplines - social and developmental psychology, history, cross-cultural psychology, experimental psychology, and psychopathology."*

[For a business management perspective, see the Yale School of Management paper titled The Ripple Effect: Emotional Contagion In Groups]

Can any of us honestly say we haven't experienced emotional contagion? Even if we ourselves haven't felt our energy drain from being around a perpetually negative person, we've watched it happen to someone we care about.

Mark 11:24 Therefore I tell you, whatever you ask for in prayer, believe that you have received it, and it will be yours.

We've noticed a change in ourselves or our loved ones based on who they or we spend time with. We've all known at least one person who really *did* seem able to "light up the room with their smile," or another who could "kill the mood" without saying a word. We've all found ourselves drawn to some people and not others, based on how we *felt* around them, in ways we weren't able to articulate.

So, Robert's choice makes sense if he is concerned about the damaging effects of emotional contagion. But... that still leaves one big issue: is "catching" only positive emotions a Good Thing? Does this mean surrounding ourselves with "fake" goodness and avoiding the truth? Does surrounding ourselves with "happy people" mean we shut down critical thinking skills?

Happy People

The notion of "Happy People" was tossed around in the Robert-Lost-His-Mind posts as something ridiculous at best, dangerous at worst. One blogger equated "happy people" with "vacuous". The idea seems to be that "happy people" implies those who are oblivious to the realities of life, in a fantasy of their own creation, and without the ability to think critically. The science, however, suggests just the opposite.

Neuroscience has made a long, intense study of the brain's fear system--one of the oldest, most primitive parts of our brain. Anger and negativity usually stem from the anxiety and/or fear response in the brain, and one thing we know for sure--when the brain thinks its about to be eaten or smashed by a giant boulder, *there's no time to stop and think!* In many ways, fear/anger and the ability to think rationally and logically are almost *mutually exclusive*. Those who stopped to weigh the pros and cons of a flight-or-fight decision were eaten, and didn't pass on their afraid-yet-thoughtful genes. Many neuro-scientists (and half the US population) believe that it is exactly this fear! = Rational thought that best explains the outcome of the last US presidential election... but I digress.

Happiness is associated most heavily with the *left* (i.e. logical) side of the brain, while *anger* is associated with the *right* (emotional, non-logical) side of the brain. From a Society for Neuroscience article on Bliss and the Brain:

"Furthermore, studies suggest that certain people's ability to see life through rose-colored glasses links to a heightened left-sided brain function. A scrutiny of brain activity indicates that individuals with natural positive dispositions have trumped up activity in the left prefrontal cortex compared with their more negative counterparts."

In other words, **happy people are better able to think logically.**

And apparently happier = healthier:

"Evidence suggests that the left-siders may better handle stressful events on a biological level. For example, studies show that they have a higher function of cells that help defend the body, known as natural killer cells, compared with individuals who have greater right side activity. Left-sided students who face a stressful exam have a smaller drop in their killer cells than right-siders. Other research indicates that generally left-siders may have lower levels of the stress hormone, cortisol."

Mark 11:24 Therefore I tell you, whatever you ask for in prayer, believe that you have received it, and it will be yours.

And while we're dispelling the Happy=Vacuous myth, let's look at a couple more misperceptions:

"Happy people aren't critical." "Happy people don't get angry." "Happy people are obedient." "Happy people can't be a disruptive force for change."

Hmmm... One of the world's leading experts in the art of happiness is the Dalai Lama, winner of the Nobel Peace Prize in 1989. Just about everyone who hears him speak is struck by how, well, *happy* he is. How he can describe--with laughter--some of the most traumatizing events of his past. Talk about *perspective...*

But he is quite outspoken with his criticism of China. The thing is, he doesn't believe that criticism *requires* anger, or that being happy means you can't be a disruptive influence for good. On happiness, he has this to say:

"The fact that there is always a positive side to life is the one thing that gives me a lot of happiness. This world is not perfect. There are problems. But things like happiness and unhappiness are relative. Realizing this gives you hope."

And among the "happy people", there's Mahatma Gandhi, a force for change that included non-violent but oh-most-definitely-disobedient behavior. A few of my favorite Gandhi quotes:

In a gentle way, you can shake the world.

It has always been a mystery to me how men can feel themselves honored by the humiliation of their fellow beings.

But then there's the argument that says "anger" is morally (and intellectually) superior to "happy". The American Psychological Association has this to say on anger:

"People who are easily angered generally have what some psychologists call a low tolerance for frustration, meaning simply that they feel that they should not have to be subjected to frustration, inconvenience, or annoyance. They can't take things in stride, and they're particularly infuriated if the situation seems somehow unjust: for example, being corrected for a minor mistake."

Of course it's still a myth that "happy people" don't get angry. Of course they do. Anger is often an appropriate response. But there's a Grand Canyon between a happy-person-who-gets-angry and an unhappy-angry-person. So yes, we get angry. Happiness is not our only emotion; it is simply the outlook we have chosen to cultivate because it is *usually* the most effective, thoughtful, healthy, and productive.

And there's this one we hear most often, especially in reference to comment moderation--"if you can't say whatever the hell you want to express your anger, you can't be authentic and honest." While that may be true, here's what the psychologists say:

"Psychologists now say that this is a dangerous myth. Some people use this theory as a license to hurt others. Research has found that "letting it rip" with anger actually escalates anger and aggression and does nothing to help you (or the person you're angry with) resolve the situation.

It's best to find out what it is that triggers your anger, and then to develop strategies to keep those triggers from tipping you over the edge."

And finally, another Gandhi quote:

"Be the change that you want to see in the world."

If the scientists are right, I might also add,

Be *around* the change you want to see in the world.

Remember the flight attendant's advice... you must put on your own oxygen mask first.

*We all possess a **Midas Touch**, a unique ability to manifest prosperity*

The psychology of money

This is the first of a fourteen-part series that explores the core tenets of Get Rich Slowly.

A dear friend of mine had a group of old high-school friends over to his home last weekend. As the daylight faded and the cool of the evening settled, they sat around moonlit swimming pool talking about life. They shared the good things They had done over the past twenty years and the bad. Inevitably, the conversation turned to money.

One woman confessed that she's a shopaholic. When she feels stressed, she buys things, something I call "shopping therapy." To prevent her husband from finding out, she's the one who pays the bills.

Another woman has more clothes than she will ever wear. Her closets are packed so full that she's begun to pile new purchases on the floor but still she buys more. My theory on this is she is unfulfilled.

One of my friends admitted that he's sunk thousands of dollars into online video games. After his divorce, he spent years addicted to his computer. (He's now turning things around: He quit gaming cold-turkey, he is re-discovering old acquaintances new friends and exercise.)

I told my own story of how I used to buy books, clothes

and self help audio book discs compulsively. "I'd bring them home, load them to my iPods, and use the information to form new techniques," I said. "I still do this only now in a more focus driven, results focused manner because I need the act of contribution. It gives me a sense of power, I guess."

Each of us had a story about how we'd done dumb things with money. In every instance, these dumb things were the product of some psychological or emotional impulse. We weren't acting rationally. We're all intelligent folks when we were in high school together, we were in the college-prep classes together and we understand the mathematics of our choices, but we made them anyway. Why?

Because smart money management is more about mind than it is about math.

The psychology of money

For years, the "expert" advice on personal finance has assumed that we act like machines, that we will always choose the mathematically optimal option. I've read countless personal finance books filled with advice that is technically correct, but which forgets the role our minds play in making financial decisions.

When discussing this notion that financial success is more often influenced by personal psychology than by mathematical ability I frequently cite Dave Ramsey's debt snowball. It's the perfect example of what I mean.

Critics of Ramsey are quick to point out that the math of his method doesn't make sense. Going strictly by the numbers, it's better to pay down debt by starting with the obligation that has the highest interest rate. The critics are right, of course, but they miss the point. In

Mark 11:24 Therefore I tell you, whatever you ask for in prayer, believe that you have received it, and it will be yours.

most cases, if we were being rational, we wouldn't have accumulated the debt in the first place. Most of the time, debt isn't a math problem it's a psychological problem. Because of that, Ramsey's method pay off the lowest balances first makes more sense. It allows quick wins, which provide positive reinforcement, which provides a motivation to continue.

Here are some of the many other ways in which our minds play a role in money management:

Any time we loan money to family or friends, emotion plays a role. And inheritances? In the past year, I've had three people tell me nightmare stories about families that have disintegrated while fighting over a parent's estate. These are psychological and emotional battles, not battles about math.

Marketing (and advertising) is the science of persuasion. It purposefully influences our spending habits even if we think it doesn't. When we reduce our exposure to advertising, it's easier to spend less.

I am in constant awe of what parents spend on their children. They want what's best for their kids, and most of them aren't afraid to pay for it. But it's not rational to buy clothes at Baby Gap instead of at Goodwill.

A lot of financial planning is about teaching the client to take emotion out of investing. Too many people make investment decisions based on psychological reactions to the economy and the stock market. It's these emotional reactions that cause people to buy high and sell low.

> Every financial goal we set is based on our personal psychology, on emotion.

There's a burgeoning body of research that explores the many ways in which money management is more mental than mathematical. "Behavioral finance" and "behavioral economics" are explored in books like Why Smart People Make Big Money Mistakes and How to Correct Them (my review), Why Smart People Do Stupid Things With Money, Predictably Irrational, Nudge, also Your Money and Your Brain.

Take back your brain

We can never completely remove the emotional and psychological aspects of money management. Nor do I think we ought to. We're humans, not robots. But I do think it's important for us to reduce the negative emotional financial decisions as much as possible. Here are some of the best ways that I have learned to combat poor choices to take back my brain:

Reduce exposure to advertising. Many people believe they're unaffected by advertising. Many people are wrong. As much as you can, avoid advertising. Watch less television (or watch it in a way that cuts out commercials). Skip magazine ads. Use an ad blocker for your browser. The less advertising you see, the less you'll be persuaded to buy things you do not need.

Avoid temptation. When I was paying off my debt and trying to reduce my spending, I forced myself to stay away from bookstores and comic shops. I knew that I lacked discipline. Rather than put myself in the path of temptation, I steered completely clear of it. If you're tempted at malls, stay away from malls. If you often succumb to peer pressure, don't go out for drinks with your friends. Stay away from the things that tempt you.

Automate. One of the best ways to trick your mind is

to simply take it out of the equation. If you find it difficult to make smart financial choices, remove the choice. Sign up for auto-bill pay. Set up an automatic monthly transfer from your checking account to your savings account. If you have access to an employer-sponsored retirement plan, take advantage of it. When you make things automatic, you cannot be sabotaged by emotion or psychology.

Practice mindfulness. When you're tempted to make a purchase, pause. Take thirty seconds to ask yourself if you truly need the thing you're about to buy. If it's a big purchase, force yourself to wait thirty days. Track every penny you spend so that you become aware of your weaknesses.

Read. Better education has helped me fight some of my mental flaws. The more I read about stock market investing, for example, the more convinced I am that making regular investments into index funds is the only way that I'm going to be a successful investor. It takes the emotion out of the equation.

I'm not sure what will happen with the friends I saw last weekend. Maybe some of them will continue to make the same financial mistakes. Maybe some of them will turn things around.

But I do know this: The answers to their problems will not come from a better understanding of compound interest or another explanation that it's important to spend less than you earn.

While these concepts are important, they're purely mathematical. In order for my friends to manage their money, they need to go beyond math they need to master their minds. When you master your emotions you are in control of your life to live life on your terms.

Mark 11:24 Therefore I tell you, whatever you ask for in prayer, believe that you have received it, and it will be yours.

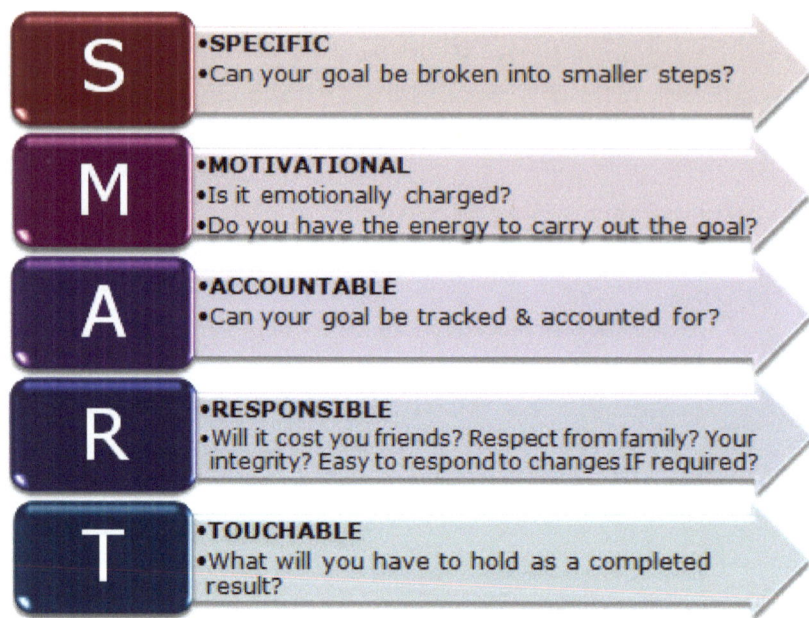

Goals Are the Gateway to Financial Success

The Road To Wealth Is Paved With Goals

This is the second of a fourteen-part series that explores the core tenets of Get Rich Slowly.

Yesterday I completed my first my first century of this season. It didn't happen exactly as I'd planned, but it happened. Instead of simply cycling 100 miles, I arrived late which means I started late and got on the road in the last of the pack. Some might view this as a failure. Not me, I'm ecstatic to have finally for the first time finish 100 miles in less than 5 hours, I met one of my first cycling goals ever.

Though I had hoped to begin at the front of the start line as usual and finish in the lead, circumstances beyond my control like traffic, GPS rerouting, etc.

Mark 11:24 Therefore I tell you, whatever you ask for in prayer, believe that you have received it, and it will be yours.

prevented my "perfect picture." Instead, I focused on my outcome, realized this is a first world problem and recognized that my biggest problem is someone else's greatest blessing. Though it didn't happen the way I intended, I accomplished my goal.

What does my cycling experience have to do with personal finance? Everything. The journey to financial success is not a race; you are not going to get rich quickly, but a ride so enjoy the journey with all of its imperfections. It doesn't matter how swiftly you pay off your debt or save for retirement. The important thing is to actually make the effort. If you don't start, you can never finish. To know where you're going, you need to set goals.

Goals are the building blocks of success

I used to be lukewarm about goals. I'd set them, but could never seem to meet them. They seemed so far away, so difficult to reach. Or a few months would pass and the goals that had once seemed so appealing no longer really mattered to me. So I then became an aimless overachiever accomplishing many conquests without reaching my outcome. I lived life without intention.

As a result, I came to view myself as inadequate. I had always wanted to be a professional strategist even though I rarely took the steps necessary which resulted in my lack of direction. I wanted to retire early, but instead I was deep in debt and digging deeper. Without goals, I wandered aimlessly through life.

Over the past few years, however, I've come to understand that goals are the building blocks of success. Goals provide direction. <u>They help you drive your life toward the things that matter most.</u>

Mark 11:24 Therefore I tell you, whatever you ask for in prayer, believe that you have received it, and it will be yours.

Since starting Get Rich Slowly, I've set a variety of financial goals. In nearly every case, I've met or exceeded my own expectations, often by a leaps and bounds. For example:

I set a goal to pay off an 185,000.00 debt within five years. I eliminated approximately $45,000.000 in debt in just 24 months.

I set a goal to make $25,000.00 a year from my consulting. Instead, I make 25,000.00 per month consulting coaches and consultants.

I set a goal to fully-fund my Roth IRA every year. I've also been able to set up and fund (to various degrees) a self-employed 401(k).

Setting these goals was not enough. I had to work at them. Sometimes the work was hard. But without having set the goals in the first place, I would never have been able to achieve them. I would still be wandering blindly in the financial desert. I would still be working at working, deep in debt, spending my entire earnings, and wondering when things would get better. Now I do what I love and I love what I do.

Review: Since I'm researching this subject right now for my book, let's review what makes a good goal. A good goal is a SMART goal. That is, a smart goal is Specific (the goal is not nebulous, but indicates precisely what you intend to do), Measurable (the goal is quantifiable instead of vague), Achievable (the goal makes you stretch, but is not impossible to reach), Relevant (the goal is meaningful to you and your situation), and Timed (the goal has a specific time by which you intend to complete it).

Mark 11:24 Therefore I tell you, whatever you ask for in prayer, believe that you have received it, and it will be yours.

The power of intention

In 1951, William Hutchinson Murray wrote the following about setting and pursuing goals:

Until one is committed, there is hesitancy, the chance to draw back. Concerning all acts of initiative (and creation), there is one elementary truth, the ignorance of which kills countless ideas and splendid plans: that the moment one definitely commits oneself, then Providence moves too.

All sorts of things occur to help one that would never otherwise have occurred. A whole stream of events issues from the decision, raising in one's favor all manner of unforeseen incidents and meetings and material assistance, which no man could have dreamed would have come his way.

I learned a deep respect for one of Goethe's couplets: "<u>Whatever you can do, or dream you can, begin it. Boldness has genius, power and magic in it!</u>"

From my experience, this is absolutely true. The "law of attraction" is an extension of God's spoken promise of ask and ye shall receive, I also believe that when you commit your entire self to the pursuit of a goal, you begin to notice unexpected chances and opportunities.

The road to wealth is paved with goals

Setting financial goals is no different than setting other goals. It's important to take all goal setting seriously, to put some thought into the process. Here are some techniques, some of which I've shared before, for setting smart financial goals:

Determine what is important to you. Money doesn't

bring happiness; pursuing goals and experiences that are aligned with our personal values brings happiness. How can you be sure your spending is aligned with your personal values?

By setting goals, I've had great success using George Kinder's three questions to crystalize what is important to me. This, in turn, helps me set meaningful goals.

Look forward, not back. Base your goals on the future, on what you want to accomplish, not on where you've already been. This forces you to think outside the box. Don't worry about past failures. Concern yourself only with what you want to accomplish in the future.

Take one step at a time. It's vital to break large goals into smaller ones. If you focus too much on the Big Picture, you may become intimidated and give up. You eat an entire meal one bite at a time so too with goals. Once I decided to pay off $185,000 in debt, I shifted my focus from the big number to the smaller steps along the way. I made incremental progress. If you're pursuing a big goal, break it into small components.

Keep your goal in mind. One way to do this is to advertise to yourself, perhaps using the techniques described at Take Back Your Brain. Regularly remind yourself of why you're doing the things you're doing, but don't obsess over the Big Picture.

Use an accountability partner. In June, GRS reader Kinley shared her system for meeting financial goals. She and her sister serve as accountability partners for each other. They've shared their current financial situation and future goals. Every month, they review their progress together.

Mark 11:24 Therefore I tell you, whatever you ask for in prayer, believe that you have received it, and it will be yours.

An accountability partner, whether sister, friend, or spouse can help you keep on track.

Be patient. Progress toward your goal can seem slow at first, but will gain momentum with time. Things will get easier. You'll learn new techniques. You may receive support from unexpected sources. Together, these things will help to accelerate your success.

Don't let setbacks derail you. It can be discouraging when your goal seems to have been stunted. You save a $5,000 emergency fund only to have your car totaled by an uninsured driver. You start a new business and a big-name competitor moves in down the street. You get your debt snowball rolling and your credit card company changes your terms. When setbacks happen, reprogram your brain to recognize the opportunity in the challenge and if you make mistakes, just get back on the right track. Persevere.

Tip: I've recently become a fan of a specific technique for tracking short-term goals I learned from GRS-reader Erica. She keeps a list of daily goals in a spiral-bound notebook. I've modified her system for my own use. Every day I make a list of the things I want to do. As I complete a task, I cross it off the list. When I think of something new that needs doing, I add it to the list. At the end of the day, I copy all of the uncompleted tasks to a new page, listing them in order of priority. This simple system has revolutionized my productivity.

Goals made simple

I think maybe Chris Silva said it best while we were walking the track a few days ago. We were at the three-mile track on Ft. Sill Military reservation when he remarked:

Mark 11:24 Therefore I tell you, whatever you ask for in prayer, believe that you have received it, and it will be yours.

You should define your goals and align your spending around them. If you get clear about what you value and not anyone else believes you should value you'll accomplish more and live a happier life.

I liked this so much that I stopped to write it down. (Yes, I carried pen and paper with me while walking I also do this on the bicycle because this is where my greatest ideas are born) Goals are important because they are the gateway to financial success.

Get Rich Slowly By Spending Less Than You Earn

I learned the hard way that this is not rocket science, The first thing we learn after counting is adding and subtracting though the concept is easy to understand it is not so easy for everyone to abide by, What is the amount of our national Debt? This is an important part of the equation and knowledge, and especially useful when teaching our little ones.

Spend Less Than You Earn

This is the third of a fourteen-part series that explores the core tenets of Get Rich Slowly.

"Annual income twenty pounds, annual expenditure nineteen and six, result happiness. Annual income twenty pounds, annual expenditure twenty pounds ought and six, result misery." Charles Dickens, David Copperfield

When people ask me for my most valuable tip on personal finance, they're often disappointed because

Mark 11:24 Therefore I tell you, whatever you ask for in prayer, believe that you have received it, and it will be yours.

my number one tip isn't a very sexy one. "To get out of debt and to build wealth," I say, "you must spend less than you earn." People are hoping for something more, some sort of mystical or magical secret. Guess what? As mundane as it sounds, that is the mystical secret of money. I will add a variable of personality discipline, what do I mean by this? When I first began my business I felt as though I was the only one who could clean, organize and file according to my standards so the result of this was I wasn't placing my energy where I excel best thus hence slowing financial growth so even though I couldn't afford a maid, accountant or assistant I hired all three placing the only option as success because I had to pay them resulting in over all success because I was now putting all of my focus in my business and I learned to delegate for productive leverage freeing up my "green time" for income producing activities which also gave me time freedom to enjoy sharing quality time with my daughter.

If you want to get out of debt and build wealth, all you ever need to do is spend less than you earn. Everything else we talk about at Get Rich Slowly is window dressing, a prop in support of the fundamental equation of personal finance:

WEALTH = WHAT YOU EARN – WHAT YOU SPEND

The wider the gap between what you earn and what you spend, the more financial success you'll achieve.

Spend less

This simple formula has a couple of implications. The first is that being frugal can have a very real impact on your financial situation. Frugality is an important part of personal finance because when you decrease your expenses, your cash flow has only one option and that is to increase. If you're living paycheck to pawnshop to finance company and repeating the process because you have more month than money then you will appreciate what I have to say here. On a $3000 a month income, reducing your monthly expenses by $300 can give you substantial breathing room. (See the Charles Dickens quote at the beginning of this article.)

The big advantage of thrift is that you can implement it immediately. In theory, if there were no psychological factors and we all know there are because all decisions are made by emotions, once you learn to master your emotions you will be in control of your future which means it is then you will live life on your terms (conquer your mind because where the mind goes the body will follow), you could cut your expenses in half today and your savings would skyrocket. Making frugal decisions and altering your spending behavior by shopping at consignment shops and goodwill instead of Dillard's or Macy's, conserving by eating out less and preparing leftovers or even going on a ramen noodle budget pays immediate dividends.

The disadvantage of frugality is that there's a limit to what you can do. You can only trim so much from your budget before you become miserable or until you don't have enough for food and shelter. If you earn $3000 a month, you only have $3000 total you can cut. At $3000 monthly income, your maximum positive cash flow is $3000.

Earn more

Thrift has limits. You cannot spend less than zero. On the other hand, there is theoretically no limit to how much money you can earn. Frugality is important, but if you want to make real progress, increase your income.

In the 4 1/2 years I've been running this site, I feel like I've never been able to make this point emphatically enough. The people I know who have met with wild financial success have all done so by increasing their income in some way. They've all had to make sacrifices to do this, but once they've met their goals, they're able to scale back to a normal way of life. If you want to destroy your debt not just defeat it, but destroy really it do something to boost your income. How do you earn more money?

Work longer hours.

Get a second job.

Start a small business.

Sell the stuff you have.

All of these options will work and yes, they all require sacrifices, especially the sacrifice of time. Most people feel that these options aren't right for them. If that's the case, if you've already cut your spending to the bone and you're unable to earn more then there's really no answer other than extreme frugality and patience.

There are no silver bullets. There's no magical way to change the fundamental equation of personal finance: To build wealth, you must spend less than you earn. If a person has already cut her/his spending to the bone and is unable to increase her/his income, she/he will continue to struggle.

Mark 11:24 Therefore I tell you, whatever you ask for in prayer, believe that you have received it, and it will be yours.

Three Financial Formulas You Need to Know and Understand

If you can remember and understand the following three financial formulas, you'll be well on your way to building wealth. They're not complicated, they're not fancy, but they will put you ahead of 90% of the population. Well, I don't really know that 90% figure is true, but it sure seems that way!

Formula One: The Debt Formula

2 − 3 = **DEBT**. If you spend more money (represented by the 3 piles of money) than you earn (represented by the 2 piles of money), you will go into debt. There is no way around it. Spending even one dollar more than you earn is bound to lead to financial destruction if carried out over a long enough period of time.

Formula Two: The Broke Formula

Once again in simple terms, 2 − 2 = **BROKE**. If you spend every penny you make, you will be broke. There is no way around it. You will be living paycheck-to-paycheck until you can break the cycle and begin following Formula Three.

Formula Three: The Wealth Formula

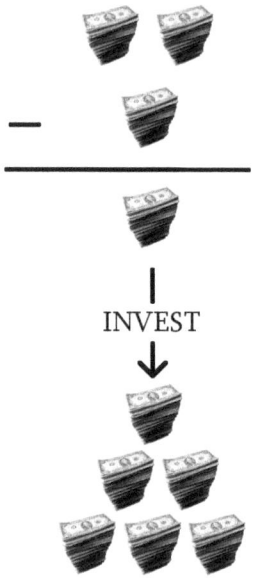

OK, this one is a little more complicated, so pay attention! 2 − 1 =**SAVINGS**. If you spend less than you earn, you'll have money left over to save. If you take that savings and invest it, you get **WEALTH**. How do you invest it? There are numerous ways, but here are a few:

4. Pay off debt! at some point debt will become your friend and it will be needed for your taxes, for now let's just get rid of it.
5. Invest in yourself and always pay yourself! (Education & Training)
6. Invest in the Stock Market! (In a low-cost, tax-efficient, diversified portfolio)
7. Invest in Real Estate! (People will always need a place to live and businesses always need a storefront!)

Mark 11:24 Therefore I tell you, whatever you ask for in prayer, believe that you have received it, and it will be yours.

8. Invest in a Money Market account, CD's, etc. for a sleep at night factor
9. Start a Business! (Probably the best option if you have entrepreneurial skills and a good business idea)
10. Take the profits and create a dream bucket for your wants and desires with the knowledge that you can only buy what you can afford from the money in your dream bucket.

That's All the Math You Need!

Well, there is one other formula you'll need to understand, compound interest. We'll talk about that later though. For now, just figure out how you can start following The Wealth Formula if you're not already. Oh, and don't spend any more time trying to figure out other financial formulas just yet. This will be all you need for a while!

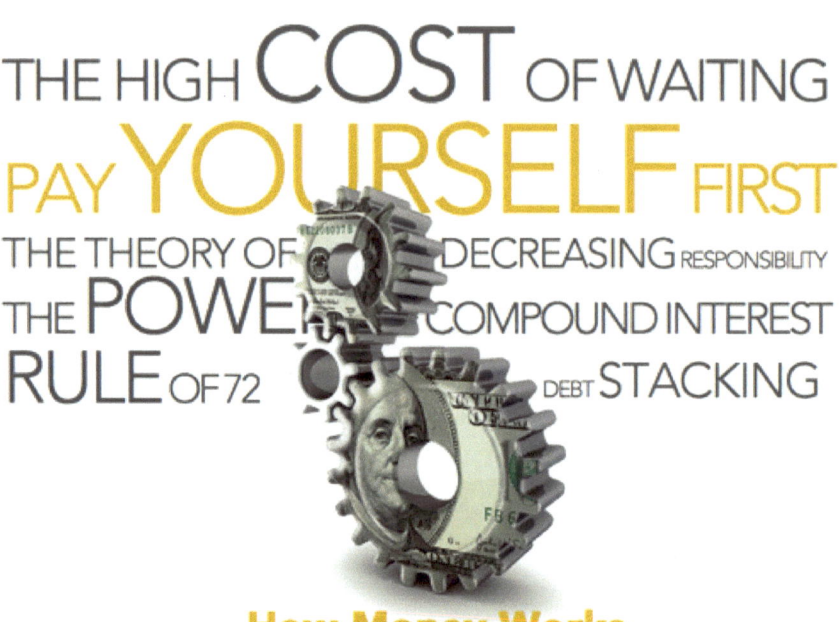

Pay Yourself First

This article is the fourth of a fourteen-part series that explores the core tenets of Get Rich Slowly. It's also a part of National Save for Retirement Week.

One of the oldest rules of personal finance is the simple admonition to pay your self first. All the money books tell you to do it. All the personal finance blogs say it, too. Even your parents have given you the same advice.

I know from personal experience it's hard. That money could be used someplace else. You could pay the phone bill, you could pay down debt, or you could buy a new DVD player. You've even tried once or twice in the past, but it's so easy to forget. You don't keep a budget, so when payday rolls around, the money just finds its way elsewhere.

Mark 11:24 Therefore I tell you, whatever you ask for in prayer, believe that you have received it, and it will be yours.

And besides: What does "pay yourself first" even mean?

To pay yourself first means simply this: Before you pay your bills, before you buy groceries, before you do anything else, set aside a portion of your income to save. Put the money into your 401(k), your Roth IRA, or your savings account.

The first bill you pay each month should be to yourself. This habit, developed early, <u>will help you build tremendous wealth.</u>

Why pay yourself first?

If you're just getting started in the Real World, saving may seem impossible. You have rent, a car payment, groceries, and maybe even student loans. Sure, you'd like to save money, except there's just no money left at the end of the month and that's the problem: Most people save what's left over, meaning, left over after bills and after discretionary spending.

If you don't develop the saving habit now, there are always going to be excuses disguised as reasons to delay: you need dental work, you want to go to Mexico with your friends, or you just aren't making enough to pay your bills.

Here are three reasons to start saving now instead of waiting until next year (or the year after or even the year after that):

When you pay yourself first, *<u>you're mentally establishing saving as a priority, this means YOU are a priority and until you see yourself as a priority no one else will.</u>* You're telling yourself that you are more important than the electric company or the landlord. Building savings is a powerful motivator and it's

Mark 11:24 Therefore I tell you, whatever you ask for in prayer, believe that you have received it, and it will be yours.

empowering.

Paying yourself first *encourages sound financial habits*. Most people spend their money in the following order: bills, fun, saving. Unsurprisingly, there's usually little to none left over to put in the bank. But if you bump saving to the front i.e. saving, bills, fun then you're able to set the money aside before you rationalize reasons to spend it.

By paying yourself first, *you're building a cash buffer with real-world applications*. Regular steady contributions are an excellent way to build a nest egg. You can use the money to deal with emergencies. You can use it to purchase a house. You can use it to save for retirement. Paying yourself first gives you freedom because it opens a world of opportunity.

I've never met anyone who does not wish they had started saving earlier. Nobody tells himself or herself, "Saving was a mistake." No matter what your age, begin saving now. And if you already save, consider boosting how much you set aside each month.

How to pay yourself first

The best way to develop a saving a habit is to make the process as painless as possible. Make it automatic. Make it invisible. If you arrange to have the money taken from your paycheck before you receive it, you'll never know it's missing.

Part of your savings plan will probably include retirement, but you should also save for intermediate goals too, such as buying a house, paying for a honeymoon, or purchasing a new car. Here are three easy ways to begin doing this yourself:

If your employer offers a retirement plan, such as a 401(k) you must enroll as soon as possible, especially if the company matches your contributions. Matched contributions are like free money.

Starting a Roth IRA is one of the smartest moves a young adult can make. These accounts allow your investments to grow tax-free. Because of the extraordinary power of compound interest (and compound returns), regular investments in a Roth IRA from an early age can lead to enormous future wealth.

Open a high interest savings account at a bank like ING Direct or FNBO Direct. Set up automatic transfers into this account, either directly from your paycheck or from your regular bank account.

Treat these transfers like you'd treat any other financial obligation. This should be your first and most important bill every month.

The real barrier to developing this habit is finding the money to save. Many people believe it's impossible. But almost everyone can save at least 1% of his or her income. That's only one penny out of every dollar.

Some will argue that saving this little is meaningless. But if a skeptic will try to save just 1% of his income, he'll usually discover the process is painless. Maybe next he'll try to save 3% or 5% as his saving rate increases, so his nest egg will grow.

If you're struggling to find money to save, consider setting aside your next raise for the future. As your income increases, set your gains aside for retirement and savings. Once you're contributing the maximums to your retirement (and you've built emergency savings), you can begin to use your raises for yourself

Mark 11:24 Therefore I tell you, whatever you ask for in prayer, believe that you have received it, and it will be yours.

again.

Sure, this means your effective salary will stagnate for a year or three or five. But it also means you'll force yourself to develop the saving habit.

Example: My former husband and best friend Chris is a perfect case study. He started by having 8% of his pre-tax income set aside in his employer's retirement plan. As Chris' salary increased, he increased the amount he saved, routing it to various retirement accounts.

Because he never saw the money in his paycheck, he never missed it. Now he saves 30% of his income, and he even receives a 6% employer match! How did he do this? By paying himself first. (I should note that Chis just came to me the other night for advice on how to save even more. Chris is awesome.)

No matter what your age, you should make it a priority to develop a regular saving plan. Establishing this habit early can lead to increased financial security later in life. But even those of us who got a late start should do our best to pay ourselves first. I didn't begin doing this until just a few years ago. Better late than never.

Though many personal finance books briefly explore the idea of paying yourself first, David Bach's 2003 bestseller, The Automatic Millionaire is devoted exclusively to the subject.

Mark 11:24 Therefore I tell you, whatever you ask for in prayer, believe that you have received it, and it will be yours.

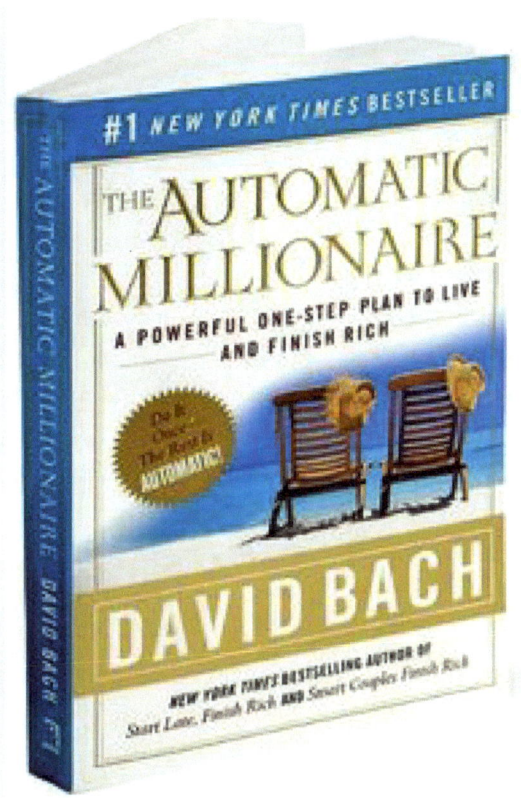

The entire book is a step-by-step guide to developing the saving habit and making it automatic. If you'd like more ideas about how to make this work in your life, this is the place to look. Any good public library will have a copy.

There are some great guidelines in this book about how much you should save for retirement.

Pay yourself first, my friends. It's a habit that you will never regret.

Mark 11:24 Therefore I tell you, whatever you ask for in prayer, believe that you have received it, and it will be yours.

Small Changes, Big Results

The Small Stuff Really Matters

This article is the fifth of a fourteen-part series that explores the core tenets of Get Rich Slowly.

Getting started with smart personal finance isn't always easy. It's one thing to read about the steps you should take, it's another thing to actually do them. Your debt is so overwhelming or your saving goals seem so lofty that you begin to believe that the only way you'll ever get where you want to be is by winning the lottery.

Part of the problem is that we live in a society that idolizes the Big Winner. Nobody celebrates the guy next door who bikes to work, grows his own food and cooks his own meals, shops at the thrift store, and gets all his books from the library. That sort of life isn't glitzy. Yet it's that sort of life that can (and does) lead to true wealth.

Mark 11:24 Therefore I tell you, whatever you ask for in prayer, believe that you have received it, and it will be yours.

Starting small

I can still remember the first thing I did when I decided I was tired of being buried in debt, have you ever seen a penny, dime or some denomination of change in the parking lot on your way to your vehicle or as you are walking along? Of course you have, I started picking those up and placing them in a jar and it is amazing how fast that money grows. I still do that to this very day, even if I am on my bicycle headed to the refuge. Sometimes I will see a dime, penny, etc. at a stop light or in the middle of nowhere and I will pick it up put it in my jersey and thank God even as I put it in the jar upon my arrival home because I believe that if you do not respect money it will not respect you and you will forever be a slave to the money instead of the money working for you.

When I became concerned about my finances, it was months before I had any big decisions to make even though there were tons of small changes I made everyday that led to big results.

It's true that it's important to save money on the big stuff, like a home or a car. Any time you make a large purchase, your opportunity to save is magnified. However the large transactions are rare. How often do you spend more than $100 on anything?

You have more opportunities to save when shopping for groceries. You can clip coupons, buy in bulk or shop for store brands or compare unit pricing. And you can do it today. Saving fifty cents a week on almond or coconut milk might be inconsequential as a one-time occurrence, however, over the course of a year, it amounts to $26. Taken together, many such small economies make a real difference. It's these small changes that will lead to big results.

Mark 11:24 Therefore I tell you, whatever you ask for in prayer, believe that you have received it, and it will be yours.

Maybe you save fifty cents a week on laundry detergent by using a less expensive brand, save $4 a week by clipping coupons, save $2 a week by riding a bicycle to work on Fridays, save $25 a month by dropping to basic cable, save $47/year by canceling your subscription to a magazine or two, and save $100 during the summer months by growing your own vegetables. These are small changes, and these choices alone would save you over $750 a year.

Remember: A penny saved is far more than a penny earned. You earn pre-tax dollars, yet you spend after-tax dollars. So what does this mean to you? Well, depending on your tax bracket, you might have to earn $111 or $133 or even $150 to actually put $100 in your pocket.

Assuming you're in the 25% tax bracket, saving $750/year is like giving yourself a $1000 raise!

Starting small has an interesting side effect. As you get in the habit of cutting costs on one thing, you find that you can transfer that skill to other parts of your life. One small step leads to another.

An uncertain future

Some folks frown on frugality. They equate it with being "cheap" and consider it beneath their dignity. Others are unwilling to make sacrifices today when the future is so uncertain. They're not willing to "live like that" when they could get hit by a bus tomorrow. I think this is crazy for a couple of reason:

First, spending is not the same as happiness. Second, most of us are likely to live a long time and with advances in medical sciences we are expected to live a very long time. Which would you rather do?

Mark 11:24 Therefore I tell you, whatever you ask for in prayer, believe that you have received it, and it will be yours.

Prepare for a long life by saving and investing, and then die tomorrow.

Spend money you don't have now, and then be unable to afford what you need when you're older.

Recently, I had a chat with an acquaintance who runs an adult foster home. She told me anecdotes about her elderly residents who've run out of money. Their quality of life is not high. If you think it's a burden now to give up your cell phone or to take the bus, try having to pinch pennies on necessities when you're 70. Or 80. Or 90.

Remember: *Don't confuse frugality with depriving yourself*. If pinching pennies makes you feel lousy, then loosen up. Spend a little more. I am not advocating "retail therapy" or spending above your means what I'm telling you is that it's okay to spend more for your favorite brand of yogurt or to get your favorite cut of beef. If you don't like shopping in thrift stores, don't.

There's real value in boosting your income, I don't deny that, I strongly believe frugality is an important part of personal finance, too. And for each of us it's different, I might be able to cut back on clothing and transportation and still realize I'll probably always spend a lot on food. On the other hand, food may be a perfect place for you to cut costs because you're not willing to compromise on your wardrobe.

Frugality doesn't mean living like a pauper. Frugality is a good thing. Thrift is a responsible choice. When we restrict our spending on the unimportant, we're able to indulge ourselves on the things that matter most in our lives.

Mark 11:24 Therefore I tell you, whatever you ask for in prayer, believe that you have received it, and it will be yours.

Don't Confuse Frugality With Depriving Yourself

Jonni McCoy's Miserly Moms: <u>Living on One Income in a Two Income Economy</u> lists eleven miserly guidelines designed to help families reduce expenses. The first of these is: Don't confuse frugality with depriving yourself.

This is the most important aspect of being successful at saving money. If any money-saving activity makes you feel cheap or tight, you will eventually abandon your efforts. That is not the price we need to pay to reach our goals.

If you have adopted a lifestyle of thrift or frugality, you are not being cheap when you buy generic food at the grocery store. You are not being cheap when you don't purchase Tide or the latest trend. You are not being cheap you are choosing a different set of values. You are working toward a greater goal. You are not depriving yourself, you have elected to live debt-free, or to follow a spiritual ideal, or to save for a trip around the world.

When you adopt a frugal lifestyle, you change your value system. You acquire less Stuff, but you gain more time, more freedom, more peace-of-mind. Making any lifestyle change through acquiring a frugal mentality, beginning an IRA or starting a diet, requires that you keep your goal in mind constantly.

If you lose track of why you are making sacrifices, the sacrifices become a burden.

McCoy recommends that you track your success as you work toward your goal. Make a chart to graph your savings effort because what gets measured gets achieved. Keep statistics on how much extra money you

Mark 11:24 Therefore I tell you, whatever you ask for in prayer, believe that you have received it, and it will be yours.

save by walking to the store instead of driving. Compete with yourself to see how small you can get your grocery bill. McCoy also advises that frugality does not mean deprivation:

When I first started my frugal lifestyle, I feared what it would involve. I believed that frugal people lived undesirable lives: wearing stained or torn clothing or reusing plastic wrap. I refused to participate in any of that. But such a definition of a frugal lifestyle does not have to be yours. There are many different degrees of frugal lifestyles. I was determined to maintain a sense of class and still be frugal.

I've said this before: Frugality isn't an all-or-nothing proposition. There are different degrees, and it's important to find what works best for your budget and your situation. Keep your eye on the goal and make conscious choices that make you happy. Don't bankrupt your future for gratification today and don't live so abstemiously that you cannot enjoy life now.

Mark 11:24 Therefore I tell you, whatever you ask for in prayer, believe that you have received it, and it will be yours.

Size Really Does Matter

Large Amounts Matter Too,

Are You Penny Smart, Pound Foolish?

This article is the sixth of a fourteen-part series that explores the core tenets of Get Rich Slowly.

A few years ago Chris re-financed his mortgage. In one simple decision, he trimmed his monthly payments for principal and interest from $1050.60 to $650.50, boosting his cash flow by $400.10 per month.

If he had consumer debt, that's $400.10 per month he could have used for his debt snowball. It's $400.10 per month he could stick in his retirement accounts, or to put into savings accounts for his trip to Germany next year or to pursue other hobbies and interests. Really, it's $400.10 he could use for anything he wanted. (As it happens, he chose to use that money to accelerate his mortgage payments.)

Note: Jamie Walkingstick gave a guest post on this subject in September when she described how she and her husband are sweating the big stuff. They made a big change that saved them $1,000 a month.

There's no question that frugality is an important part of personal finance. It's good to clip coupons and to mend broken furniture and to turn the thermostat down, it's even better to shop around for the best deal on a mortgage.

Everyday frugality can save you a little money consistently, but by making smart choices on big-ticket items, you can save thousands of dollars in one blow. Or you can boost your cash flow by hundreds of dollars per month.

Some people spend so much time sweating the small stuff that they don't bother to do the same on the big stuff.

They're penny wise and pound foolish, negating their daily scrimping and saving by making poor financial decisions that burden them for years. Chris has a co-worker who once bought an SUV for $43,000. After a year, he decided to trade it in, but could only get $23,000 for it. Ouch!

Now obviously, you only get a few chances in your life to save big on a home or a car. You rarely make financial decisions involving tens (or hundreds) of thousands of dollars.

However, you probably do make other big decisions several times a year. You buy a camera or a television or a new piece of furniture. You book a cruise or fly home for Christmas or hire somebody to work on your house.

These are prime opportunities to save money. Whenever you anticipate a big expense, you should look for ways to maximize the value you get for your dollar.

As I've shared before, here are the guidelines I use to steer my shopping for big-ticket items:

Mark 11:24 Therefore I tell you, whatever you ask for in prayer, believe that you have received it, and it will be yours.

Know what you want before you start. If you're buying a vacuum cleaner, what are you going to use it for? What features do you need in a television? What features do you want? When I bought a small digital camera in 2007, I jotted a quick wish list: wide-angle lens, large display, easy-to-use menu, and superior video quality. Some of these items (like superior video quality) were much more important than others.

Set a budget. Ideally, you'd set a budget for your purchase before you started shopping. That's not realistic. You can't know how much a dishwasher costs until you actually look at a few. But once you have a sense of the landscape, decide how much you're willing to spend.

If you don't set a budget to start, it's easy to succumb to "desire inflation". When shopping for my digital camera, I had a budget of $800.

Research your options. Once you've created a features list and a budget, search for options that meet your requirements. In most cases, Consumer Reports is a great place to start. Your local public library probably has a copy of the annual Consumer Reports Buying Guide. But don't discount the web. I often do product research through Amazon.

Make a selection. Once you've done your research, you'll probably find one or two items that seem most promising. (There's rarely one perfect choice.) I tend to write down the manufacturer and model number of my top three choices before I move on to the next step. In 2007, I was able to narrow my choices down to two camera models, both of which were within my budget.

Compare prices. Now that you have a shortlist, begin researching prices. Again, check Amazon. Check other

Mark 11:24 Therefore I tell you, whatever you ask for in prayer, believe that you have received it, and it will be yours.

online vendors. Check your local stores. Don't forget to consider used or refurbished items.

Make the purchase. Once you find the best source for the item you want, buy it. Be confident that you've researched price and features so that you know you're getting a good deal.

Protect your investment. The older I get, the better I am about saving warranty information and boxes. (If I had a smaller house, I'd only save boxes for a couple weeks. Because I have space above the garage, I save them forever.) A little foresight when you buy a product can save a lot of headache down the road.

But large amounts don't just matter when you're refinancing your house or shopping for a new plasma TV. One of the best ways to discover the power of large amounts is through boosting your income. Whether that's through negotiating your salary, asking for a raise, or changing careers, a larger income can have a huge impact on your finances.

Remember: Saving money on the little things every day is great, but saving money on the big things can make an awesome difference to your budget.

Money Make-Over Budget

Do What Works for You

This article is the seventh of a fourteen-part series that explores the core tenets of Get Rich Slowly.

I struggled with debt for over a decade. I made several attempts to tackle the trouble, but nothing seemed to work.

Compulsive spending was part of the problem, I bought anything I wanted, even if I couldn't afford it, and there was another factor, too.

> Everything I'd read gave the same advice for debt reduction: Start by paying off your highest-interest rate debt. I understood the logic behind this, but I couldn't make it work. The trouble was that my highest-interest rate debt was also my debt with the biggest balance (a fully-maxed $16,000 credit card at 21% interest). I'd plug away at this for several months at a time, but then give up because it felt like I was never getting anywhere.
> Then I read about the debt snowball approach in Dave Ramsey's <u>The Total Money Makeover</u>.

Mark 11:24 Therefore I tell you, whatever you ask for in prayer, believe that you have received it, and it will be yours.

> It blew my mind. Here was somebody saying that it was okay (good even) to do something different, to start by paying low balances first. I tried it, and 39 months later I had eliminated over $185,000 in consumer debt.
>
> In the process, I learned a valuable lesson. In order to succeed with money, sometimes you have to ignore the conventional wisdom. Sometimes you simply have to do what works for you.

The perils of dogmatism

There's too much dogmatism in our culture. People are convinced that their way is the right way to do things. I don't begrudge those who are certain they're right. When something works for you, you have a tendency to believe it's the right choice for everyone else, so you preach it with fervent passionate. I understand that.

The problem, of course, is that we're all different. Your religion, your politics and your financial tips work for you, but won't necessarily mesh with my situation and experiences. And mine won't fit with yours. There are few one-size-fits-all solutions in personal finance, or anywhere else.

For example:

As I hinted earlier, there's no right way to pay off debt. Yes, you'll save a little if you tackle the high-interest stuff first, but you may have better chances of success by starting with low balances instead.

There's no right way to invest. I like real estate, but you might prefer individual stocks.

Mark 11:24 Therefore I tell you, whatever you ask for in prayer, believe that you have received it, and it will be yours.

There's no right way to tackle your mortgage. Some experts recommend paying it off quickly; others recommend stretching it out as long as possible to take advantage of the low interest. The best choice is the one that best matches your goals for the future.

There's no right way to be frugal. Some folks are unwilling to sacrifice organic groceries, and others are unwilling to take the bus. That's fine. Find ways to practice thrift that fit your lifestyle.

Joint or separate finances, this can get confusing if you are not in alignment with your goals? There is no right answer. Just because you can't conceive that a couple can have a strong relationship with separate finances doesn't mean that it's impossible. Millions of people do it with no problems.

There's no right way to budget. Some people use a loose framework to guide their spending. Others need detailed line items. The best budget is one that you'll actually use.

There's no single best savings account, checking account or credit card. There are plenty of great choices. Don't listen to anyone who says you're wrong for choosing a good option that works the way you do. (I feel great about using ING Direct, even if they don't offer the highest rates because it works for my outcome.)

When the belief that there's just one right way to do something traps you, you set yourself up for failure: If this "right" method doesn't work for you, you have no other options. You have to keep using it, even if you keep failing. Now it's time to change your blueprint for

Mark 11:24 Therefore I tell you, whatever you ask for in prayer, believe that you have received it, and it will be yours.

new financial directions.

If you allow yourself to consider other options, you give yourself multiple pathways to power insuring success. Yes, you could use the "right" method, or you could take a different path to reach the same goal.

Doing what works

I'm not saying that it's okay to do anything you feel. It's not okay to keep on spending just because dealing with your debt is difficult or uncomfortable. I am saying it is okay to try something new when what you're doing doesn't work, and it's okay to ignore the naysayers who complain that you're "not doing it right". You want to find what works for you, not for somebody else.

Don't listen to anyone who tells you there's just one right way to do something. Each person is different. What works for one person may not work for another. Be willing to experiment until you find methods that are suited to your life.

Make informed choices, understand the consequences, and focus on your goals.

Do what works for you.

6 Attitudes That Breed Financial Failure

Financial success or failure is often the results of attitudes, both conscious and unconscious, that affect our behavior. No amount of budgeting and self-control can help us when we're up against ingrained ideas about money management, spending, and debt.

If you're having a tough time shifting your financial behavior, maybe it's time to change your mind about money. Here are six common attitudes that work against us financially.

1. Stuff Is Just as Good as Money

Besides a few important exceptions like our home, car, and other necessities, objects are seldom as valuable as cold hard cash. When you trade your hard-earned money for objects, don't fool yourself into thinking they retain even an approximation of their retail value for very long. Typically, by the time we file our receipts, depreciation, changing styles, or new technology has reduced our treasures to trinkets.

2. I'll Start Saving When I Make More Money

There's no optimal time (or salary range) to begin the good habit of saving. Setting your course early in life, regardless of how much money you make, establishes a routine and habit that can be tweaked as your financial realities and goals change. Many people tell themselves "I don't make enough to save," but isn't the flip side of that "I make so little that saving is essential"?

3. Time Is on My Side

The Twenty-something's may disagree, but time really does fly. Saving early and often will compensate for most financial mishaps. The twin powers of habit and compounding interest can make huge nest egg from even the most modest income.

4. Little Things Don't Count

Volumes have been written about the "latte factor," and various savings gurus argue the point ad nauseum. I'm not a proponent of total self-denial, but there's something to be said about how our little habits and mini indulgences can, if left unchecked, add up to big expenses. Understanding how our own personal latte factor (whatever it might be) erodes our larger financial goals is important first step in becoming more savings savvy.

5. Debt Is No Big Deal

Everybody carries some sort of debt, right? Wrong. Simply put, most debt is draining, and there's real freedom to be found in avoiding it. Besides the interest, the worry, and the depletion of readily available cash resources, debt limits our opportunities and that is a big deal.

With the exception of a home and education, seriously consider how consumer debt is foreclosing on your options. What choices would you make if you didn't have debt? If you could do it all over again, what debt would you avoid? Do you still emotionally embrace debt even while being intellectually against it?

6. My Lifestyle Should Constantly Improve

We live in a society where the arrow on the chart is always expected to head north. We've even come to see consistency or stasis as some sort of warning sign.

Companies are expected to cut costs and make more money; consumer spending should increase quarter after quarter; factories are expected to expand. Even our homes should grow, as we trade that "starter home" for something larger.

What's wrong with a bit of satisfaction in what we already have? Why can't our lifestyles, after a certain point, remain relatively constant as we work toward our financial security? Maybe it's time to embrace debt-free living as the ultimate new luxury item.

When we change our attitudes about money, we change our relationship with it. And when we recognize how culture is a big part of how we're conditioned to think about our finances, we can slowly start to shift that thinking. In short, the quickest and most powerful thing we can do to reinvent our financial lives is change our minds.

Pace Pace Wins The Race

Slow and Steady Wins the Race

This article is the eighth of a fourteen-part series that explores the core tenets of Get Rich Slowly.

One reason I got into financial trouble during my early twenties was that I wanted everything right now. I looked at what my parents had, and it occurred to me that they'd been working their entire lives to get to financially nowhere because they had the attitude that "you can't take it with you" resulting them in spending whatever little money they earned which wasn't much because they only spoke Cherokee.

I wanted a heightened level of comfort, and I wanted it now. I wanted what I saw in the magazines and on TV. I wanted to start at the end, not the beginning.

In order to afford that sort of lifestyle, I went into a lot of debt. What I learned was that I couldn't manage that

Mark 11:24 Therefore I tell you, whatever you ask for in prayer, believe that you have received it, and it will be yours.

lifestyle for very long without what I called "tide in, tide out" and even that wasn't what I wanted. I lived high on the hog for a couple of years, and then found myself back in the Real World, but with lots of extra bills to pay.

In an attempt to reach the "finish line" of life sooner, I'd put myself further behind.

It wasn't until a decade later that I finally understood that patience and perseverance are crucial to success, with money and everything else.

Patience and perseverance

There are those who get rich quickly. People do win lotteries. They do sign sports contracts or get "discovered" by Hollywood or sell their small businesses to big conglomerates. And some are able to profit from risk and luck, picking the right stock at the right time, so that their $10,000 investment grows into a million.

These things happen. But these chosen few represent a tiny fraction of all those who achieve financial success.

More typical is the story of my neighbor, a real millionaire next door. He worked hard for thirty years or more, practiced frugality, and invested wisely. He wasn't rich when he was young, but he enjoyed life while doing all of the "right" things.

He was patient, and eventually this patience paid off. Now he's able to do what he wants without worrying about money.

Getting rich slowly doesn't mean you have to give up everything you love. Reducing your expectations and

Mark 11:24 Therefore I tell you, whatever you ask for in prayer, believe that you have received it, and it will be yours.

desires doesn't mean you can't spend your money on the magazines you enjoy, bicycles, motorcycles or Prada shoes.

It simply means recognizing that you can't have everything you want. And often, you'll have to wait for the things you do get.

Small steps become big strides

Personal finance can be daunting. When you first tackle your debt, the numbers are overwhelming. When you think about how much you need to save for retirement, you might ask yourself how it's even possible. And when you think about having to work every day for the next 30 or 40 years, you may feel a pit in your stomach.

You can accomplish big things if you break them into small pieces. Last week, I rode Spin Your Wheels. If I'd focused on how long 100 miles actually was, or how hot the weather was going to be (over 100 degrees), or the possibility of heat exhaustion, I never would have started. Instead, I set a target pace, and I tried to meet that pace every single mile.

The same applies to personal finance. For example:

You can't expect to go from $20,000 in debt to having $20,000 in the bank overnight. It takes time. You get out of debt one month at a time, one payment at a time. You get out of debt by sticking with it. Wealth is built the same way.

Although it's important to take advantage of opportunities to save big, you should also do what you can to save on the small stuff. Big wins come along infrequently, but there are many opportunities to "sweat the small stuff".

Mark 11:24 Therefore I tell you, whatever you ask for in prayer, believe that you have received it, and it will be yours.

Given time, these small habits have a huge cumulative effect, and they can lead to financial prosperity.

You can devote a lot of time to trying to pick the right stocks and timing the market for the best time to buy. But even the experts fail at this more often than they succeed. Instead, most financial advisers (and even billionaires like Warren Buffett) recommend that average folks take the "slow and steady" approach: Use dollar-coast averaging to make regular small investments in indexed mutual funds.

Instead of expecting to accomplish everything at once, recognize that meaningful change takes time. Be patient. Work hard. If your experience is like mine (and that of many GRS readers), you'll find that after a few months (or years), you're not only making progress, you're making more progress than you believed possible.

Your slow and steady movements have become large, graceful strides.

The biggest loser

My former husband Chris is Biggest Loser fan. Every season, the program follows a group of contestants as they attempt to lose weight by reversing a lifetime of bad choices.

In one episode last spring, contestants were challenged to pull NASCAR vehicles around a race track. The muscular men sprinted to an early lead. Meanwhile, former model Tara Costa, who had demonstrated patience, perseverance, and drive every week, put her head down and pulled at a moderate pace.

The men tired. They began to flag, but Tara's pace

Mark 11:24 Therefore I tell you, whatever you ask for in prayer, believe that you have received it, and it will be yours.

never faltered. One-by-one, she passed the jackrabbits and coasted to victory.

Tara, in green, steadily passed Mike and gained on Sione

I think of this challenge often. It seems to epitomize so much of what I've learned about life, and personal finance. As Tara pulls her car, she doesn't worry about what the people around her are doing. She sticks to her game plan, moving slowly but surely toward the finish. Just as in the fable of the tortoise and the hare, slow and steady really can win the race.

(And, as a final note, I'll point out that you're only racing with yourself, not anyone else.)

Perfection vs. Outstanding

"Striving for excellence motivates you; striving for perfection is demoralizing."
— Harriet Braiker

The Perfect is the Enemy of the Good

This article is the ninth of a fourteen-part series that explores the core tenets of Get Rich Slowly.

You want the best for yourself, for your spouse, for your family. You want the best car, the best house and mortgage, the best job, the best mutual funds, and the best savings account. You want things to be perfect. We all do. Perfection does comes with a price and is the lowest standard you can set for yourself because the only perfection is imperfection with all of it's beauty.

Research has shown that those who are obsessed with perfection are more likely to have physical and mental problems than those who are open-minded and flexible. Perhaps worst of all, perfectionism costs time and lots of it, trust me as a perfectionist I know.

To find the best option whether it's the best dishwasher or the best mortgage broker can take days, weeks or months. (And sometimes it's an impossible mission.)

The pursuit of perfection is an exercise in diminishing returns:

Some initial research will teach you the basics.

A little more research will help you separate the wheat from the chaff.

More research yet will enable you to make an informed decision.

Theoretically, if you had enough time, you might find the perfect option.

But each unit of time you spend in search of higher quality offers less reward than the unit of time before it. Here's a graph of how time spent researching affects the quality of your decisions:

Quality is important. You should absolutely take time to research your investment and buying decisions. Just remember that perfect is a moving target, one that's almost impossible to hit. It's usually better to shoot for "outstanding" today than to aim for a perfect decision next week.

Procrastination is one common consequence of pursuing perfection: You can come up with all sorts of reasons to put off establishing an emergency fund, to put off cutting up your credit cards, to put off starting a retirement account. But most of the time, your best choice is to start now.

Who cares if you don't find the best interest rate? Who cares if you don't find the best mutual fund? You've found some good ones, right? Pick one. Get in the game. Just start. Starting plays a greater role in your success than any other factor.

When you spend so much time looking for the "best" choice that you never actually do anything, you're sabotaging yourself. The perfect is the enemy of the good.

Failure Is The Key To Success

Failure is Okay

This article is the 10th of a 14-part series that explores the core tenets of Get Rich Slowly.

The ability to keep going in the face of failure is critical to success when learning any new skill to include learning to manage your money. Nobody's perfect. We all make mistakes with money every day. I've made tons in the past, and I continue to make them. Here are just a few examples:

I managed to take on over $185,000 in consumer debt before turning things around.

I tried (and failed) to repay my debt several times before stumbling on the debt snowball method, which worked for me.

Before I embraced the idea of mutual funds, real estate and CD's I repeatedly poured money into stocks that tanked.

Mark 11:24 Therefore I tell you, whatever you ask for in prayer, believe that you have received it, and it will be yours.

I could name dozens of other examples big and small. But the key is every time I realize I've made a financial mistake, I learn from it so I don't repeat it in the future. Sometimes I do repeat my mistakes on a smaller scale only now I fail forward.

Building success from the ashes of failure

In Failing Forward, John C. Maxwell writes that there are seven key abilities that allow successful people to overcome failure instead of taking each setback personally. Successful people:

Reject rejection. Successful people don't blame themselves when they fail. They take responsibility with the ability to respond for each setback, they don't take the failure personally.

View failure as temporary. "People who personalize failure see a problem as a hole they're permanently stuck in," writes Maxwell, "achievers see any predicament as temporary."

View each failure as an isolated incident. Successful people don't define themselves by individual failures. They recognize that each setback is a small part of the whole.

Have realistic expectations. This one is huge. Too many people start big projects such as paying off their debt with the unrealistic expectation that they'll see immediate results. Success takes time. When you pursue anything worthwhile, there are going to be bumps along the way. And remember: The perfect is the enemy of the good.

Focus on strengths. This was one of the biggest lessons I took away from Tim Ferriss' The 4-Hour

Workweek. When I interviewed Ferriss last year, I asked him to expound on this idea. He told me: "Focus on leveraging and amplifying your strengths, which allows you to multiply your results. Fix any fatal weaknesses to the extent that they prevent you from reaching your goals, keep in mind perfection isn't the path to your objectives; finding ways to cater to your strengths is."

Vary approaches. "Achievers are willing to vary their approaches to problems," Maxwell writes. "That's important in every walk of life, not just business." If one approach doesn't work for you, if it brings repeated failure, then try something else. Maxwell is saying that to fail forward, you must do what works for you, not necessarily what works for other people.

Bounce back. Finally, successful people are resilient. They don't let one error keep them down. They learn from their mistakes and move on.

These seven points form a firm foundation for dealing with failure in all parts of life, including personal finance. As you pay off your debt, as you learn to invest, as you cut your spending, accept that some failure is inevitable. This does not mean you are not your mistakes. Own them, learn from them, and move on. (And remember: Good habits keep small mistakes manageable.)

It's never too late to change direction, to start making smart choices. If you're 40 and don't have retirement savings, you can start saving tomorrow. If you're 30 and staggering under the weight of credit card debt, you can cut up your cards and make a commitment to change direction. The wonder of the future is that it can be built upon the ashes of the past.

Mark 11:24 Therefore I tell you, whatever you ask for in prayer, believe that you have received it, and it will be yours.

At 45, I can look at who I am and can connect the dots back through my life. Though I do not regret saving for retirement when I was younger, though I do not regret accumulating massive credit card debt, though I do not regret living a consumerist lifestyle, I do now see that these experiences made me the woman I am today. Without them, I wouldn't be motivated to help others make smart money decisions. (And let's be clear: I am not advocating that others repeat the mistakes I've made.)

Failure is okay

Embrace fear as a tool to serve you rather than a prison that holds you in bondage from enjoying life in all of its glory. Step out of your comfort zone, take on new adventures, mitigate risks and enjoy the journey, if you don't experience the things you are scared of, if you don't risk failure you will never succeed.

If you've made poor financial choices, don't let them get you down. Don't let them make you afraid to live again. Draw from your experience, fall down seven times, get up eight.

Mark 11:24 Therefore I tell you, whatever you ask for in prayer, believe that you have received it, and it will be yours.

The Art Of Financial Balance

Financial Balance Lets You Enjoy Tomorrow and Today

This article is the 11th of a 14-part series that explores the core tenets of Get Rich Slowly. It originally appeared at Soul Shelter in a slightly different form.

For more than a decade, I was buried in debt. My relationship with money was a one sided love affair because I had zero respect for money. I earned a decent income, better than most and somehow I still couldn't seem to get ahead. I lived paycheck-to-paycheck on a

Mark 11:24 Therefore I tell you, whatever you ask for in prayer, believe that you have received it, and it will be yours.

salary that anyone could thrive on.

I'd frequently find myself standing in a store, holding a stack of audio books, or maybe several magazines. Inside, I'd be arguing with myself, almost as if there were an angel on one shoulder and a devil on the other. Most of the time, the devil won. I'd buy the stack of CDs or the magazines by making reasons that they were necessities instead of luxuries and I would more often than not be broke waiting for the next paychect. I was a compulsive spender.

Eventually, two friends helped me to realize the path I was on. I began to read personal finance books, I started with Think And Grow Rich, I converted to the "lifestyle" of frugality. I learned to pinch pennies.

This newfound thrift was exactly what I needed. It helped me to get out of debt and to begin building wealth. I even opened my first "real" savings account, I have now built a sizable emergency fund. Best of all, I'm maxing out my retirement savings every year.

Going to extremes

Something happened along the way. As I converted from spendthrift, thrift, my relationship with money changed, it didn't improve. I went from a woman who spent too much to a woman who spent too little.

Again, it took outside intervention for me to realize I had a problem. A few years ago, I complained about the cost of movies. I complained about the cost of groceries, etc. I even complained about the cost of hot chocolate. "You're not being frugal," a close friend told me. "You're being cheap."

That was a wake-up call. I realized that I was still

struggling to develop a healthy relationship with money. I hadn't achieved balance.

And balance is what's required. I believe that thrift is a virtue, and I refuse to abandon it, thrift can also be a vice if taken to an extreme. It's not wrong to spend money on yourself, when you can afford it. Money will work for you to serve the greater good when you decide to quit being a slave to it, money should be used to bring us joy, when possible.

The balanced money formula

One tool that I've embraced for the past few years is the balanced money formula introduced by Elizabeth Warren and Amelia Tyagi in their excellent book, All Your Worth: *The Ultimate Lifetime Money Plan.*

Here's what it looks like:

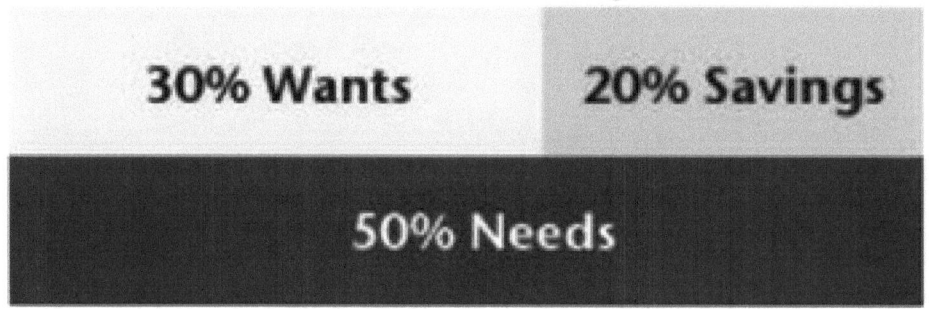

As you can see, when your financial life is in balance, you're allocating enough for savings and needs; you're also setting some aside for the things you want. This idea is simple, but it was a revelation to me. No more spending too much on wants and no more pinching pennies, either.

Mark 11:24 Therefore I tell you, whatever you ask for in prayer, believe that you have received it, and it will be yours.

Update: Oops. My original draft of this article featured a more-detailed explanation of the formula, but I edited it out because I thought we'd covered this plenty in the past. Quick review: The Balanced Money Formula uses after-tax income.

Though my fancy-pants graphic doesn't reflect it, the percentages are more properly stated as "no more than 50% on Needs" (meaning that your needs are not expected to increase with income), "up to 30% on Wants" (again, these don't have to increase with income), and "at least 20% on Savings (which includes debt reduction, emergency fund, and retirement savings). I apologize for the confusion.

Since embracing the Balanced Money Formula, I've been much happier. It's a sort of broad non-prescriptive budget the gives me the freedom to spend on my Wants, like bicycles and new cycling gear as long as I'm taking care of my Needs and setting something aside for Savings. I've learned that I can stay frugal in my day-to-day life and it's okay to splurge a little on the things I like including good hot chocolate.

Finding balance

In order to find balance, you've got to do some soul-searching. I think of it as a three-step process:

Find what makes you happy. Look inside yourself and ask, "What is it that brings meaning, pleasure, and joy to my life?" Be honest. How can you create a life that features more of the good stuff and less of the mundane?

Focus on your goals. Set personal goals based on the things that make you happy. If you like music, maybe one of your goals could be to learn to play the guitar. If you want to change careers, maybe one goal would be to go back to school. Make meaningful goals a priority, and let the other stuff be secondary.

Seek balance. Strive for moderation in all things. Pursue your goals, but don't forget frugality. Be frugal, but don't forget your goals. Work hard to build your financial fortress while allowing yourself to have a little fun, too.

The quest to achieve financial balance is about more than money. It's also about meaning. Money is important, yes, just remember it's not the only thing. Money is a means, not an end and success without fulfillment is failure

Each of us has parts of our lives that feel unbalanced. When we experience this lack of equilibrium, it's important to do something about it, to make changes. From my experience, however, the most effective changes are small they're incremental. When we overcompensate for an imbalance, we sometimes just make ourselves miserable in a different way.

Sleight Of Mind, Seeing Through The Illusion

Nobody Cares More About Your Money Than You Do

This article is the 12th of a 14-part series that explores the core tenets of Get Rich Slowly.

I've read a lot of stuff lately about how scammers take advantage of other people. (Example, here is a brief summary of seven psychological tricks con artist use.)

(Excerpt from Lloyd Morgan)

Seven Psychological Principles Con Artists Exploit

Inherent human vulnerabilities need to be taken into account when designing security systems/processes, suggests a study that looks at a dozen confidence tricks from the UK TV show "The Real Hustle" to determine recurring behavioral patterns con artists use to exploit victims.

This study was a carefully constructed collaboration between Frank Stajano of the University of Cambridge Computer Laboratory and Paul Wilson, writer and producer of the aforementioned TV show (Wilson was an IT consultant for twelve years before moving into entertainment).

The seven principles of human behavior that con artists exploit, according to the article:

The distraction principle: While you are distracted by what retains your interest, hustlers can do anything to you and you won't notice.

The social compliance principle: Society trains people not to question authority. Hustlers exploit this "suspension of suspiciousness" to make you do what they want.

The herd principle: Even suspicious marks will let their guard down when everyone next to them appears to share the same risks. Safety in numbers? Not if they're all conspiring against you.

The dishonesty principle: Anything illegal you do will be used against you by the fraudster, making it harder for you to seek help once you realize you've been had.

The deception principle: Things and people are not what they seem. Hustlers know how to manipulate you to make you believe that they are what they want you to perceive.

The need and greed principle: Your needs and desires make you vulnerable. Once hustlers know what you really want, they can easily manipulate you.

The Time principle: When you are under time pressure to make an important choice, you use a different decision strategy. Hustlers steer you towards a strategy involving less reasoning.

NOW BACK TO THE ORIGINAL ARTICLE

It's easy to think that those who lose their money are just unfortunate suckers. That's not always true. The most intelligent people are more likely to fall victim, the less intelligent individuals are least likely to become a victim of manipulation because they use more common sense than logic.

On some level, the same thing happens all the time with bankers, brokers, and real-estate agents. Even with friends and family these folks may not be con artists, we've all at some point allowed these other people to tell us what we should do with our money. We let ourselves believe that they're able to make better decisions about our financial situation than we are.

Sometimes they can, but more often than not, they can't or won't because the truth is, your money just isn't as important to anyone else as it is to yourself.

One of the most powerful lessons you can learn is that nobody cares more about your money than you do. When you realize this, when you take responsibility for making your own financial decisions (instead of letting others make them for you), it can bring a tremendous sense of power and control to your life.

Trust no one

If your real-estate agent says you can afford a

particular house, don't just take her word for it. Run the numbers yourself. Set your own budget for a mortgage; don't just trust the mortgage broker or the bank. Of course they think you can afford more they have commissions riding on it!

If your insurance salesman tells you that whole life is better than term, don't just take his word for it. Do your own research. Find out what's right for your situation. (Hint: It's probably term.) Of course he wants you to buy whole life he'll make five to ten times more than he would if you bought term.

If your lawyer tells you to create a living trust in addition to a simple will, don't just take her word for it. Dig a little deeper. Learn what a living trust is. Find out why people use them. Ask yourself if this makes sense in your circumstances. You may very well decide to have your lawyer create a living trust or you may decide that $800 is better spent elsewhere.

If the salesman at the Mega Mart argues that you should take out an extended warranty on your new 180" deluxe di-lithium-drive television, don't just take his word for it. He has zero motivation to give you advice that's in your best interest. His advice is based on what's in his best interest, which means more money in his pocket.

If your favorite personal-finance blogger urges you to invest in index funds, don't just take her word for it. Read up on the subject yourself. Though it's unlikely that a blogger is going to profit from your investment choices, it's very possible that her investment goals and your investment goals are different. Maybe she's well off and merely wants to match market returns. Maybe you're young and would like a little more risk. Make time too use the blogger's advice as a starting point, but

Mark 11:24 Therefore I tell you, whatever you ask for in prayer, believe that you have received it, and it will be yours.

do your own reading, your own planning, and make your own investment decisions.

When you see an ad on television, on a blog or in a magazine, don't just believe what the marketing copy tells you. Of course the latest Trends are the best! That's what all ads say, right? Big corporations don't have your best interest at heart. All they care about is the bottom line. To get the facts on quality and performance, check out impartial reviews through Amazon, Consumer Reports and your friends.

The truth is out there

Don't get me wrong. I'm not saying that it's bad to talk to a financial planner or to use a real-estate agent to buy a house. You should absolutely have a team of financial advisers. Heed the advice of experts. Listen to what they have to say. But don't follow their recommendations blindly.

The advice that others give you is almost always in their best interest, which may or may not be the same as your best interest. Never forget this. Don't do what other people tell you just because they have authority or because they have a silver tongue.

Read. Research options. Understand the pros and cons of every choice. (Because every choice will have its pros and cons.) Don't become obsessed with perfect, and be willing to make mistakes. Realize that what's right for one person may not be right for you.

And, especially, never make a financial decision under time pressure. If somebody tells you this is a limited-time offer and you need to act fast or you'll miss out, then miss out. It's almost always the best choice. (Creating time pressure is one of the oldest tricks in the

Mark 11:24 Therefore I tell you, whatever you ask for in prayer, believe that you have received it, and it will be yours.

book, and an easy way to get people to go against their own best interest.)

Know what's important to you and why. Use this knowledge to set goals. And use these goals to direct your choices. When you have a why, it's easier to trust your own judgment.

Do these things, and you'll appreciate that nobody cares more about your money than you do.

Mark 11:24 Therefore I tell you, whatever you ask for in prayer, believe that you have received it, and it will be yours.

Financial Fertility vs. Investment Impotence

Action Beats Inaction

This article is the 13th of a 14-part series that explores the core tenets of Get Rich Slowly.

Three years ago, I was a different woman. I was recently divorced, I had no savings, retirement or otherwise. I was starting over from zero because of my impotent goals coupled with the fact that I had just gone through a divorce. I was over $185,000 in debt. I just began speaking again and writing books. I spent my free time on my bicycle to free my mind, find clarity and discovered this is where I find my greatest inspiration, honesty with others and myself, it is where I find humble through my strengthened relationship with God.

Let's fast-forward to today. I have an amazing life living my dreams. I'm out of debt. I have more than $20,000 in emergency savings, I max out my retirement accounts every year, and I make more than I ever have in my life. Best of all, I earn my money doing something I love: helping others to find their passion and discover new ways to achieve it. My work is meaningful; it helps other people while I'm helping myself.

Mark 11:24 Therefore I tell you, whatever you ask for in prayer, believe that you have received it, and it will be yours.

What changed? Well, to put it bluntly, I made a decision to do what I love and to love what I do because of this I am successful. What does this mean to you? This is your recipe for success, duplicate and you too will be successful.

Overcoming resistance

It's easy to read about personal finance (or any other area of self-improvement) and to tell yourself, "Yeah. That sounds nice. I really should spend less on eating out. I really should exercise more. I really should open a Roth IRA."

It's easy to tell yourself these proven facts although few people actually follow through. They talk the talk; they just don't walk the walk. Instead, they sit on their hands, afraid to take action. They procrastinate because that's what seems easiest. (And sometimes they actively try to interfere with those who are bold enough to make changes in their lives.)

In The War of Art, Steven Pressfield writes about defeating procrastination and the other things that prevent us from fulfilling our dreams: fear, rationalization, self-doubt. Pressfield calls these dream-killers Resistance. He writes (with some formatting help from me):

Most of us have two lives. The life we live, and the unlived life within us. Between the two stands Resistance. What is your resistance? Once you identify this you will find it easy to break free from the psychological bondage and breakthrough to the life you desire.

Have you ever brought home a treadmill and let it gather dust in the attic? Ever quit a diet, a course of

Mark 11:24 Therefore I tell you, whatever you ask for in prayer, believe that you have received it, and it will be yours.

yoga, or a meditation practice? Have you ever bailed out on a call to embark on a spiritual practice, dedicate yourself to a humanitarian calling and commit your life to the service of others?

Have you ever wanted to be a mother, a doctor, or an advocate for the weak and helpless; to run for office, crusade for the planet, campaign for world peace, or to preserve the environment?

Late at night have you experienced a vision of the person you might become, the work you could accomplish, the realized being you were meant to be? Are you a writer who doesn't write, a painter who doesn't paint, an entrepreneur who never starts a venture?

If you have then you know what Resistance is.

Resistance comes from the war inside you, I call it inner conflict: from lack of confidence and fear of failure.

Action beats inaction

The best way to defeat Resistance is to actually do something, if only for ten minutes a day. Tell yourself that you'll move toward your goals for ten minutes a day. If you don't succeed, do it again. Keep going until you do succeed.

It doesn't matter if your actions are small. It doesn't matter whether your actions are "right". It doesn't matter if you make mistakes. In fact, it doesn't matter if you fail along the way. It doesn't matter if there are other "better" things you might have done. All that matters is that you do something because any action that moves you in the direction of your desired

Mark 11:24 Therefore I tell you, whatever you ask for in prayer, believe that you have received it, and it will be yours.

outcome is "on the right track" as progress only happens when a decision is made, just remember the definition of decision is to cut off, to sever, leaving no other option or alternative. Just remember the story of troy, find your driving force, your leverage, and be resolved in your commitment. You must start moving in the direction of your dreams.

You can only afford to pay off $10 per month on your credit cards? Do it.

You can only pay 1% of your income into a high interest savings account every month? Do it.

You can only put $100 into your Roth IRA instead of the full $5000? Do it.

Do what you can, and do it today. Stop rationalizing. Stop saying, "I'll do this next week". The best time to start any positive course of action is now. This isn't just New Age self-talk; it's the truth. Start saving now. Start exercising now. Start writing your book now. Start spending time with your family now.

Your life can be amazing, the only one who's going to make that happen is you.

Success, What Is Your Definition?

It's More Important To Be Happy Than To Be Rich By

This article is the final installment of a 14-part series that explored the core tenets of Get Rich Slowly.

Here's the opening paragraph from my forthcoming book, *Financial Fertility: Your Missing Money Link*. It's the sum of everything I've learned during my five year journey to get rich slowly:

You don't want to be rich; you want what you believe the money will buy you to make you happy. Many people mistakenly believe that the former leads to the

Mark 11:24 Therefore I tell you, whatever you ask for in prayer, believe that you have received it, and it will be yours.

latter. While it's certainly true that money can help you achieve your goals, provide for your future, and make life more enjoyable, merely having money doesn't guarantee happiness.

Many of us (including me) get wrapped up in the belief that having more money is the key to a better life. It's not, the key to a better life is increased happiness. For some people, that does mean more money. But according to the research Tal Ben-Shahar shares in his book Happier, most of us would be better served by:

Creating rituals around the things we love to do.

Expressing gratitude for the good things in our lives.

Setting meaningful goals that reflect our values and interests.

Playing to our strengths instead of dwelling on weaknesses.

Simplifying our lives, not just the Stuff, the time.

We're more likely to lead happy lives by putting these principles into practice than by getting another raise at work, especially if the increased income would only lead to increased spending. When we focus on monetary goals, we run the risk of becoming trapped on the "hedonic treadmill" (also known as lifestyle inflation), working harder and harder to make more and more money. This does not lead to happiness.

Sometimes money can buy happiness

Wealth and happiness aren't mutually exclusive, of course. According to financial writer Jonathan Clements, financial stability improves your well-being in three ways:

If you have money, you don't have to worry about it. By living below your means, you can obtain a degree of financial control even if you aren't rich. Avoiding debt gives you options.

Money can give you the freedom to pursue your passions. What is it you want out of life? What gives you a sense of purpose? These are the sorts of things you want to pursue in retirement. Better yet, try to structure your career around something you love to do.

Money can buy you time with friends and family. In fact, Clements says, true wealth comes from relationships, not from dollars and cents. Social capital is worth more than financial capital.

Money is a tool. As with any tool, a skilled craftsman can use it to build something amazing: a meaningful life filled with family and friends. If you're not careful, if you don't have a plan, the life you construct with your money can be a tenuous thing, even dangerous.

Lessons learned

Studies show that the pursuit of money is less likely to bring personal fulfillment than focusing on self-improvement and, especially, close relationships with others. Here are a handful of lessons I've learned during my research into the connection between money and wealth. I didn't come up with any of these ideas; they're products of actual research into what makes us happy:

People who are materialistic tend to be less happy than those who aren't. If your aim is to have more money and more Stuff, you'll be less content than others whose goals are built around relationships or mental/spiritual fulfillment. (Life will pay you what you ask of it.)

Over saving does not lead to happiness. While it's important to save for the future (and to cope with current emergencies), research shows that over saving can actually have a negative impact on your quality of life. If you're meeting your goals for saving, it's okay to spend some on the things that make you happy.

Experiences tend to make us happier than material things. We have different reactions to the money we spend on experiences and the money we spend on Stuff: When we spend on experiences, our perceptions are magnified (meaning we feel happier or sadder than when we spend on Stuff), and the feelings tend to linger longer. And since most of our experiences are positive, spending on activities instead of material goods generally makes us happier.

When we lower our expectations, our happiness increases. High expectations come when we compare ourselves to others or when advertising bombards us. We come to accept the things we see on TV as "normal", and because we don't have these things, we feel inadequate.

Our expectations rise, and before long we're caught up in lifestyle inflation. If we can consciously manage our expectations, both financial and otherwise we increase our sense of well-being.

Really, there's only one-way to ever be satisfied with how much money you have: You must define how much is enough. True happiness comes when you learn to be content with what you have. If you don't take the time to figure out what enough means to you, you'll

Mark 11:24 Therefore I tell you, whatever you ask for in prayer, believe that you have received it, and it will be yours.

always be unhappy with your financial situation.

How much is enough?

Enough looks different to each of us. It's not just different amounts of money, but different types of wealth. For me, enough is being debt free with the time freedom to travel the world to participate in the many bicycle events and to train in different environments to enrich my experience of cycling. For you, enough may mean living in a small apartment but owning a boat and having the freedom to sail for months at a time.

To find enough, you have to set goals. You have to look inside to find your morals, values and beliefs that make up your blueprint. It can take months or years to get clear on what makes a meaningful life for you, or it can take a moment to find clarity, once you've done this, you can make choices that reflect your priorities.

After all, that's why you're doing this. You're not building wealth just so you can bathe in buckets of cash. You're building wealth so you don't have to worry about money, so you can pursue your passions, and so you can spend time with your family and friends.

Remember, my friends: True wealth isn't about money. True wealth is about relationships, about good health, and about continued self-improvement. True wealth is about happiness. Ultimately, it's more important to be happy than it is to be rich because success without fulfillment is failure.

www.ingramcontent.com/pod-product-compliance
Lightning Source LLC
Chambersburg PA
CBHW041520220426
43667CB00003B/50